Henry Dyson, under the pseudon
co-author of *Living in France*, nov

French Real Property and Succession Law

A Handbook

HENRY DYSON
Solicitor

SECOND EDITION

ROBERT HALE · LONDON

© *Henry Dyson 1988*
First published in Great Britain 1988
Second edition 1991

Robert Hale Limited
Clerkenwell House
Clerkenwell Green
London EC1R 0HT

British Library Cataloguing in Publication Data

Dyson, Henry
  French real property and succession law :
  a handbook.
  1. France. Real property. Law
  I. Title
  344.4064'3

ISBN 0-7090-4499-2

Photoset in Sabon by
Derek Doyle & Associates, Mold, Clwyd.
Printed in Great Britain by
St Edmundsbury Press Ltd, Bury St Edmunds, Suffolk.
Bound by WBC Bookbinders Limited.

Contents

Introduction to Second Edition

According to recent figures available from the Institut National de la Statistique et des Etudes économiques, there are currently in excess of 45,000 British nationals who hold French Residence Permits. There is no means of knowing how many in addition own property in France but have no need of a *permis de séjour* but it is generally assumed to exceed that number substantially. There is therefore a considerable number of British nationals whose ownership of land in France is, irrespective of their domicile, in any event both during their lives and on their deaths governed by French law. As to those domiciled in France, all their assets, both real and personal and wherever they may be situate, are generally subject to the laws of France.

Nor is there any means of knowing how many of all these British owners of French assets have in the past had or will in the future have the benefit of proper advice on their transactions in France. My experience over a period of years is that either the percentage is minimal or the advice which they have been given has in many circumstances been singularly unsuitable. It goes without saying that 'proper advice' means not only advice on the effects of French law but also on the interplay of French and English law. In some cases, this lack of advice has, one must admit, been the result of hot sunshine, at least adequate if not over-sufficient wine, and an attractive girl in the *bureau de vente* when a binding contract to buy has been signed without a further thought to the results. I suggest, however, that in very many more cases, English professional advisers, be they Lawyers, Accountants, Bank Trustee Managers or others, have had due warning of what their clients had in mind and either have failed to appreciate the dangers or, perhaps not unreasonably, had not sufficient knowledge of a system of foreign law to know what were the right questions to ask of those who had.

I was brought up that the Opinion obtained from Counsel is only as good as the Instructions upon which it is based and that no Instructing Solicitor should ever ask Counsel 'to advise generally', since this was a clear indication that he had scant appreciation himself of what was the nature of the problem on which he sought an Opinion. My object in writing this book is in no sense to provide a treatise on French law. It is to provide sufficient background information to serve as initial signposts down the right roads, so that the right questions may be asked of the right people and heed taken of the pitfalls which the answers elicit. At worst, even without the questions being posed, there will be a warning of the existence of pitfalls.

I hope also that this handbook will be of interest to those unfamiliar with certain aspects of the French legal system. It being intended as a practical book, I have deliberately omitted references to statute and case law except where I have thought that the reader might wish to read the relevant articles of the Code Civil himself.

I have deliberately treated French legal problems and practice primarily from the viewpoint of an English lawyer but with, I hope, a sympathetic understanding of their French background. For example, as will be seen from Chapter 9 on Joint Ownership, the French have no problems about a choice of the type of joint ownership in which a purchase should be made; it is considered prima facie to be an offence against the family to resort to the method which circumvents its entrenched inheritance rights. Similarly, sales *en viager*, dealt with in Chapter 13, which can prove to be most advantageous transactions for both seller and buyer, are often looked on in France as deliberate attempts to deprive the family of assets. But that is no reason why the English should not make use of these techniques although it is unlikely to be the French lawyer who would advise them to do so.

Superficially, it is interesting to see translations of foreign legal documents but in fact there is little merit in providing these in a book of this nature. Literal translations usually make nonsense reading. On the other hand, to provide translations in wholly 'correct' English legal phraseology implies that the French law attaching to the wording used in the original language is the same as attaches to the English translation. Nevertheless, in a few cases there are documents whose inclusion helps to illustrate the procedure involved and where there are only minimal translation problems. I have therefore limited myself to a few precedents of documents of this kind, in Appendix A, and these appear where necessary in both English and French.

The law of every civilized country reflects the character of its citizens. Whatever defects may be found by the English in their legal system and the administration of justice in their country, both are highly thought of in other countries, and many aspects of both would (as many French lawyers admit) considerably simplify the French system and render it less hidebound. However, in order to appreciate the workings of that system, it is necessary to understand sympathetically three very typical national quirks of which French law must take account. First, no Frenchman trusts another Frenchman so that whilst the English system proceeds on the assumption that all is in order, the French system proceeds on the basis that it is not unless it is strictly proved that it is. Secondly, 'the grey area' is not a concept of French jurisprudence. What is black is black and what is white is white but what is neither black nor white is black. The reason is simple. In all cases of doubt, it is safer to say 'no'. Among other things, this leads to a disarming brevity of style in many of the Articles of the Code Civil. Finally, despite a long tradition that the French are logical, this is wholly untrue. I strongly recommend anyone who really wants to understand the French legal system through an understanding of the French themselves to read *France* by Professor Zeldin (Collins, 1983) or the chapter on the French in Luigi Barzini's *The Europeans* (Penguin, 1984).

Inevitably, comparisons made in this book are between French and English law. I trust that Scottish readers will nevertheless find the explanation of French law useful even if, trained as I am only in English law, I am unable to make any comparisons with the laws of their country. They know that the average Englishman is unaware that Scotland has its own laws and legal system; they may be more surprised to learn that the French, with whom they have perhaps rather happier historical ties than do the English, are just as liable to call the United Kingdom England and to assume that English law runs in Scotland. On the other hand, where I have referred to the United Kingdom or Great Britain, I have done so deliberately.

I have been loath to rely entirely on the Interpretation Act that the male includes the female but, as any draftsman will know, to do otherwise is to add considerably to the length and complexity of the document. So as not to give offence, I have tried to use words which cover both sexes or avoid the issue, but frequently this would impose an unacceptable burden on all involved in the publication of this book and its readers. For this, I hope I may be forgiven. The French also make the masculine include the feminine and those who remember their French grammar will recall that they are forced to go further than the English – inevitably, since adjectives must agree with subjects and one adjective cannot be made to agree with both a masculine and a feminine subject so that the masculine prevails.

Since the first edition of this book appeared, there has been a growing tendency for British buyers to look for holiday homes in parts of France where traditionally the British have never bought. It is no business of mine to question the wisdom of this trend but it has brought into play certain factors which from a conveyancing point of view are of significance. It may be that it is fortuitous that in those traditional areas to which the non-French buyer has heretofore restricted himself (and to which, with the exception of the British, he continues to restrict himself) are for the most part south of a line passing east-west through Lyons and that in those areas certain unusual conveyancing practices common in the north of the country are generally absent. It may be that contact over a number of years with foreign buyers has instilled in Estate Agents and Notaries a sophistication in conveyancing matters which their north country brothers have yet to acquire. Suffice it to say that I consider the problem to be of sufficient importance to merit special reference in a number of the chapters which I have extended accordingly.

I would like to take this opportunity to express my gratitude to Maître Chantal Pasqualini and Maître Guy

Rousseau, *Notaires associés* of Nice, and to members of their staff who, over the years, have generously imparted their knowledge of French law and notarial practice.

My thanks are also due to Joy Wotton, whose editorial patience has been unbounded and whose editorial skills wellnigh limitless.

My greatest debt of gratitude is due to my wife whose knowledge from the cradle of the French has provided me with the most profound and valuable insight into their way of life and their attitude towards problems which the Code Civil is intended to regulate.

The law stated in this book is correct as at 1 January 1991.

Note

A Glossary will be found following Appendix D. It has been prepared for the reader who is not familiar with French legal phraseology to avoid the need to resort to continuous translations and explanations in the text itself.

Part I
Real Property

1   The French Civil Code

'My true glory', said Napoleon, 'does not lie in my having won forty battles; Waterloo will obliterate all memory of such victories. What nothing can efface, what will live for ever, is my Civil Code.'

The first Code of Civil Law applicable to the whole of France came into effect on 21 March 1804 (or according to the Revolutionary Calendar still then in use, 30 Ventose de l'An XII) under the title of 'le Code Civil des Français'. In September 1807 it took the name of the 'Code Napoléon', only to be given its previous title again some ten years later. In 1852 the Code became once again entitled 'le Code Napoléon' but from 1870 was referred to simply as 'le Code Civil', by which title it is officially known today.

To what extent he was justified in claiming 'glory' for the creation of the Code Civil perhaps depends on whether one is pro- or anti-Napoleon. The introduction to a leading standard edition of the Code Civil has it that Napoleon 'anxious to see the completion of this project to which he attached the greatest importance' personally attended many meetings of the Conseil d'Etat, actively intervening in the discussions to express his own views and imposing them when necessary. On the other hand, a well-known one-time Professor of Law at the University of Paris in an article in the *Encyclopaedia Britannica* says that whilst Napoleon took part in virtually every meeting of the Conseil d'Etat in his capacity as Chairman, '... interesting as his observations occasionally are, he cannot be considered as a serious collaborator in this great work.'

It is not difficult to appreciate how desirable it had become by the eighteenth century to have a system of law standard throughout the whole of France. However, it was not until as late as the Constitution of 1791 that, following the disappearance of the *ancien régime*, the French citizen was promised a single system of law to replace the previous diversity which incorporated legal principles garnered from multiple sources many of which were applicable only on an immediate territorial basis. Even then, it was nearly fifteen years before this promise was fulfilled. As a result, in many instances, customary law replaced existing written law in use in the south of the country, so that much law previously in force in the Parisian region became effective throughout the land.

The Code, however, did not do as much as might have been expected to weld France into one country. As early as 1539, the Edict of Villers-Cotterets had required that all '... awards, judgments, and all other proceedings ... of our sovereign Courts ... registers, inquests, contracts, commissions, sentences, wills and other acts, writs ... be pronounced, recorded and delivered to the parties in the "*langage maternal françois*" and not otherwise'. Recorded in French, such public acts may have been: it is doubtful if many were transacted in French, for as late as 1863 about a quarter of the population of France spoke no French at all but only local *patois*. Indeed, it is generally acknowledged that it took the First World War and the imperative need for orders given in French to be obeyed by all rather than by only some of the Army to ensure that French became eventually, if not currently spoken throughout the country, at least everywhere understood.

As Eugen Weber says in *Peasants into Frenchmen* (Chatto & Windus, 1977), 'The Napoleonic Code, reflecting abstract urban ideas and interest ... was ... ignored for a while in certain places and ways were found to adjust its notions to local needs. On the other hand, when the conditions of work and life had changed enough, the mincing machine of the Napoleonic Code became less dangerous and in some ways more convenient.'

Until 1880, very few alterations were made to the Code. The political changes which took place in France during that period had little influence on it. Louis XVIII specifically undertook to uphold it in its then form, and there was no reason for Napoleon III to tinker with the work of his uncle.

Since that date, many amendments to the Code have been

made to take into account the important changes which have taken place in French society. Generally speaking, these amendments follow far behind the events which called for their making. New Articles on divorce were introduced in 1884 to replace those repealed in 1816 when divorce was abolished as a sop to the Church. In that year also, considerable amendments were made to better the rights of wives and children. In 1938 the succession rights of illegitimate children were revised. Later years have seen many further fundamental changes. The law on adoption, guardianship of infants, *régimes matrimoniaux*, legitimacy and again divorce has all undergone very considerable change, as has the law dealing with the various aspects of land development and companies.

It is said that the Code Civil in its original form was remarkable for its 'conciseness and precision'. It certainly has none of the flavour of the Act of Parliament. It seems in its present form to suffer less from the enormities which bad draftsmanship has from time to time inflicted on the public, but to the average non-French reader the Code can appear to provide alarmingly brief statements of law. Recourse to French textbooks tends to provide rather less interpretation than is to be found in English textbooks and rather more straight quotation of the Code with little explanation.

However, if Napoleon perhaps overstated his claim to 'glory', it is certainly true that the Code Civil which at one time bore his name has had an immense influence on many countries whose legal systems were not based on English Common Law. Certainly, until the creation of the German Civil Code at the end of the nineteenth century, the French Code Civil held a pre-eminent position at a time of the making of nations. Apart from such places as widely separated as Holland, several of the Swiss cantons, the kingdom of Naples, Danzig, the Duchy of Parma and of Warsaw to which Napoleon gave his Code in right of conqueror, by the end of that century some twenty-five countries had either newly come into existence or had attained political maturity. These include as varied a selection as Romania, Japan, Turkey and Egypt, to say nothing of the countries in South America which had won their independence from Spain or Portugal. The promulgation of a modern code of law was the touchstone of civilization for countries such as these and virtually all adopted the French Code Civil. To what extent the reasons for this choice were sentimental – in the sense that it was drawn up in the wake of a Revolution which promised Liberty, Equality and Brotherhood, that French was (although not universally spoken in France) the language of the philosopher and diplomat, that the Code was secular but not offensively so and that it was considered overall to embody all that was best in the age's spirit of liberalism – is perhaps irrelevant. The fact is that the Code Civil has stood the test of time and remains today the basis of the civil law of France and of many other countries throughout the world and is, though perhaps more out of France than in France, almost always referred to as the Code Napoléon.

2   The Notary

'To the vast majority of the French, the Notary is often considered a survival from the past. The need on many occasions to use his services, the continued use of documents overfull of old-fashioned phraseology, the payment of fees the amount of which it is often difficult to appreciate and the calculation of which is something of a mystery, all engender in the notary's clients a sense of incomprehension bordering on distrust.' In these terms, as recently as February 1987, was cast the opening paragraph of Le Particulier's number on *Le Notaire et Vous*. Until very recently the profession has done little to dispel this image, and even today the formalism of notarial documents tends to hold back rather than keep pace with modern business transactions.

The Notary's code of professional conduct is, as one would expect, very strict, being designed to conserve the independence and integrity of the profession but in some respects it seems to prohibit what would be reasonably permitted to the English Solicitor. It is for example, only since 1986 that a Notary has been allowed to become a Director of a limited liability company on the condition that he does not authenticate any document to which that company is a party. The standard French complaint that the Notary unnecessarily takes his client's money in advance or holds on to it for an overlong time in order to earn interest on it is totally untrue. Clients' moneys must be banked either at a local Banque de Consignation (which is a State bank) or in certain cases with Crédit Agricole. Neither bank pays interest but the Notary receives 1% on the funds banked 'for managing the account'. What is true is that transactions, particularly probate matters, can sometimes take what the English client would consider an unconscionable time to resolve but, to a very great extent, this is the fault of the legal system itself and there is no doubt that the profession would, for example, much benefit from the introduction of the English reliance on brother professionals' undertakings and probably also a more supple banking system.

In as much as the Notary is inevitably involved in all conveyancing and succession matters, his nearest counterpart in England is the Solicitor, but his *raison d'être* and the fact that his functions are so limited make the comparison not wholly accurate. He is, for example, never involved in contentious work. He advises but much advisory work which in England would be considered routine work for the Solicitor is often not undertaken by the Notary. However, since it will inevitably be with the Notary that contact will be had on conveyancing and probate matters in France, it is desirable to appreciate the special character of his office.

The Notary is appointed by the State '... to receive for authentication all deeds and documents to which the parties either are obliged by law or themselves wish to give the character of authenticity which attaches to 'public' documents, to guarantee the date of such documents, to conserve them and to provide certified and ordinary copies of such documents'. There are a little over 7,000 Notaries in France; of this number, about half practise on their own and half practise in partnership. A Notary or an association of which the members are Notaries is the holder of the office of Notary. Notarial associations are, in fact, a particular type of French company, the *société civile professionelle*, but this exhibits the qualities of an English partnership rather than those of an English company. A Notary who is a partner in a firm is called a *Notaire associé*. There is only a limited number of holders of the office of Notary, which can from time to time be increased or decreased by the Minister of Justice if the needs of a particular area merit it. The Notary is an *Officier Public*; that is to say, he is appointed by the State to be the holder of an office (*une charge*) for life which entitles him to authenticate documents. There is, therefore, no question of just passing the required examinations and setting up in business as a Notary. The office itself must be acquired either on a death or a retirement or on an increase of notarial offices.

To the extent only that among his other work the English

Notary Public authenticates documents prepared in or out of the country and usually for use out of the UK, can he be compared with the French Notary who, apart from exercising the functions referred to above, may be said to be an important and possibly the most successful tax-gatherer in France. The efficiency of this method of collecting the very considerable fiscal impositions which are linked to notarial transactions is ensured by the fact that the Notary incurs jointly with those who execute documents before him the liability for stamp duties, Land Registry and a variety of other impositions. For this reason, a Notary is required to obtain, prior to completing any transaction, a payment on account sufficient to cover duties, taxes and similar disbursements in connection with that transaction and a notice to that effect is always prominently displayed in the waiting area of every Notary's office. In many cases it is not possible to calculate accurately these disbursements until quite some time after completion of a transaction and it is customary for Notaries slightly to over-estimate their requirements in this respect. It is interesting to conjecture whether, since the French are a very practical people, it is for this reason as well as for the advantages which the system of authenticated documentation is said to bring that the Notary has and presumably will retain an absolute monopoly of conveyancing and probate matters in France.

The attitude of the French public to the Notary and, therefore, of the Notary to his clients is inevitably also coloured by his position as an *Officier Public* as opposed to that of the Solicitor, who is an Officer of the Court. Moreover, since he is primarily a recorder of documents (and his role as an archivist is of considerable importance), frequently he is in effect acting for more than one client, whose interests would in England be considered inevitably to be in conflict. He is therefore required not to take the side of one of the parties to a transaction against the other and always to act with a 'constant care for fairness'. The position of the Notary may therefore, on occasion, prove to be an uneasy one. Thus, if a purchaser buys property and the conveyance is executed before the vendor's Notary, no Notary having been instructed to act for the purchaser, that sole Notary has a duty to advise each party on the effect of the contents of the conveyance and the transaction generally. But there is a limit to the extent of such advice and in certain respects his duty falls far short of that normally expected of a Solicitor.

For example, a Notary is not expected of his own volition to explain the effect of all documents involved in a sale or indeed the contents of a conveyance or other document which seem clear and obvious to him but which are in the event totally meaningless to his clients. The parties before him must themselves seek explanations from the Notary, which he is, of course, bound fairly to give. Moreover, apart from such information as a Notary can obtain from the Land Registry, Local Authorities and the like, he is under no obligation to check that documents which have been given to him are complete or correct and care must be taken in this respect by the layman. On the other hand, he must, in addition to identifying the parties and their '*état civil*' (see Glossary), ensure that the document to be executed represents the agreed wishes of the parties and, if thought necessary, advise on alternative and more effective or desirable methods of achieving the same object.

It is not possible in the context of one chapter to elaborate on the professional duties and obligations of the Notary. In many respects, his professional life is governed by rules which are not so different from those which govern the professional life of the Solicitors. He is, among other things, bound by professional secrecy in all matters other than in certain tax inquiries and professional indemnity policies are obligatory. The equivalent of the Solicitors' Compensation Fund also exists.

It is, however, not unfair to say that (with obvious exceptions) the Notary is more likely to be surprised that the law operating in England is not French than is the English Solicitor to know that transactions in France are not governed by English law. This coupled with the fact that certainly in land transactions the parties (particularly if they do not reside in France) are very unlikely to see the Notary involved before the moment of completion can lead to unfortunate misunderstanding as the effect of French law which may prove very expensive to put right. With the ever-increasing amount of international work, it is axiomatic that it is desirable to establish directly or indirectly a working relationship with a Notary who has, if not a knowledge of, at least a 'feel' for the Anglo-Saxon outlook.

It is an absolute rule that a buyer of land always has choice of Notary to act for him, and this despite whatever may be expressed in the contract. An English buyer should always invoke this rule. If the seller wants to use his own Notary, it costs the buyer no more in notarial fees, which are split between the two Notaries involved. With regret, it must be said that it seems to be more common than one would expect for sellers' Notaries who are not also acting for buyers to refrain from making draft documents available to the buyer's Notary until immediately before the completion date, seemingly in the hope that in the end the buyer's frustration will result in their acting for both parties and thus obtaining a full rather than a half fee. So serious a comment would not be made if experience did not merit it. However, in all fairness to the Notary who expects to act for both parties because a buyer has for want of proper advice until late in the proceedings allowed the contract to indicate that only he is involved, buyers should be firmly encouraged to insist that any contract they sign should contain the nomination of a Notary to act on their behalf.

Notaries' fees are either *emoluments* or *honoraires* although it is common to speak loosely of both as *honoraires*. The former are fixed by scales which apply to the particular type of transaction involved; hence there are two factors involved in calculating such a fee. This method of charging is dealt with in Appendix B. The latter are subject to no scale and are fixed by agreement. In addition, where a transaction is more than usually complex or involves special knowledge or skill, the Notary may ask that a scale fee should not apply. This must be done in writing with an explanation of the special circumstances in issue and an estimate of the proposed fee or its method of calculation. It is not probable that such a situation would arise in a conveyancing matter unless the consideration is very low and it can be seen in advance that the work will be long and tedious but it may arise in probate matters. Ordinary advice given not in connection with an *acte* immediately to be executed is charged by agreement between Notary and client.

Many English Solicitors will note with envy the results of

being an *Officier Public*. Whilst it would seem that the Notary is required to behave towards his clients in accordance with very much the same code of conduct as is a Solicitor, he has a protection against his clients' behaviour not available to the Solicitor. Articles 222 to 224 of the French Code Penal provide for the offence of 'contempt' against certain State functionaries, which, since the lowest-grade policeman enjoys a similar protection, can make it inadvisable to be excessively impolite to the police as well as to the Notary. Such contempt towards a Notary which will bring the contemnor to the attention of the criminal courts may be by word or gesture, in writing or by threats and may be uttered against an individual Notary or the profession as a whole. It is as well to make justified complaints to the local *Chambre des Notaires* in due form instead, although in all probability the average policeman will react less well to deserved criticism than will the Notary to criticism which may in all probability be quite undeserved.

It is not uninteresting in the light of what has been said above to compare what is required of the Solicitor with the obligations of the Notary towards those who make use of his services. No clearer exposé of the duties of a Solicitor in the circumstances in which the non-French are likely to come across the Notary can be found than in the dictum of Bingham LJ in *County Personnel (Employment Agency Ltd. v Alan A. Pulver & Co. (1987) 1 All E R at p. 295 – 'If in the exercise of a reasonable professional judgment, a Solicitor is or should be alerted to risks which might elude even an intelligent layman, then plainly it is his duty to advise the client of these risks and explore the matter further'. The Notary's duty stops far short of that.

3   Contracts

French law does not distinguish as did s.40 of the Law of Property Act 1925 or does s.2 of the Law of Property (Miscellaneous Provisions) Act 1989 between sales of realty and of personalty. Articles 1582 and 1583 of the Code Civil read 'A sale is an agreement by which one party undertakes to deliver a thing for which the other party undertakes to pay, ... It is completed as between the parties and property in the thing sold passes from the seller to the buyer upon agreement as to its identity and price notwithstanding that delivery has not taken place nor payment made.' Hence a verbal agreement to sell, provided it embodies such essential elements as a correct description of the property and the price, is enforceable in France, though there are obvious difficulties of proof. A letter of instruction, for example, by one of the parties to his Notary to prepare the conveyance will be considered as good evidence of the existence of such a verbal contract.

Quite apart from the obvious undesirability of verbal agreements for the sale or purchase of land, no transfer of land can be validly achieved in France other than by an *acte de vente*, which is a notarial document, prepared by a Notary and signed by all parties or their Attorneys before him. No Notary will be grateful if presented with a verbal contract on which to base the *acte de vente*. It is extremely unlikely that the average French seller would attempt to sell to a non-French buyer on the basis of a verbal contract but the latter should take care to ensure that he does not inadvertently find himself bound by such a contract.

There are two types of written contracts for the sale and purchase of land currently in use in France. A third type, which is really no more than the grant of a right of first refusal (*pacte de préférence*), is not likely to be offered to a

25

non-French buyer but if it is, it requires the most careful advice, for it can contain a number of traps for the unwary, be he French or not.

Normally, therefore, such contracts will be unilateral (*promesse de vente*) or bilateral (*compromis de vente*). The former contains an offer to sell by the seller but imposes no immediate obligation to buy on the buyer, who has a limited time in which to accept the offer to sell; upon acceptance of that offer (*levée de l'option*), the contract becomes binding on both parties. The latter is a form of contract such as is currently in use in England, i.e. its execution by both seller and buyer binds both parties from that date onwards, subject to such conditions as it may contain. In fact, as will be seen, the *promesse de vente* is treated as not strictly unilateral since a buyer under this type of contract is usually subjected to certain obligations, although these do not include an obligation to buy.

As to the French view on the use of one or other of these two types of contract, Maître Jean Picard, author of *Technique de la vente d'immeuble* (Litec, Paris), says: 'It cannot be denied that there is a complete division of opinion among Notaries. On the one hand, some prefer the *promesse de vente* despite its imperfections and its inconveniences; on the other hand, there are those who only use the *compromis de vente* as the form of contract to bind seller and buyer.' He then spends a chapter on discussing the pros and cons of the two types of contract.

From a practical point of view in the south of France, where the vast majority of British buy, the *compromis de vente* is almost exclusively used. The *promesse de vente* is much more used in country districts and in the north. Over the whole country, about 40% of contracts are prepared by Estate Agents and 60% by Notaries, but this division of labour must be redefined for the British buyer since in the south and in the large towns throughout France almost all contracts are prepared by Estate Agents, whilst in the country Estate Agents are very thin on the ground. The best advice is that the foreign buyer who is used to a bilateral contract should endeavour to have a *compromis de vente* but if the seller insists on a *promesse de vente*, the buyer should require it to be prepared by the seller's Notary and submitted in draft to his Notary.

The following points are peculiar to the two main types of written contract:

Promesse de vente

1. It may be in the form of either a notarial or a non-notarial document. All such contracts, if they are s.s.p., prima facie become void if they are not submitted for stamping within ten days of the exercise by the purchaser of his option. This is primarily an anti-tax-avoidance provision since a notarial *acte* must in any event be stamped within one month and registered at the Land Registry within two months of execution. However, there are many instances in which the terms of the contract are such that this rule has been held not to apply, such as where a buyer has paid a substantial deposit or has agreed to pay a penalty if he does not exercise his option.

2. The offer by a seller to sell, so long as it remains unaccepted by the buyer, can be withdrawn unless he has undertaken not to withdraw it for a stated period. If no such period is mentioned, the offer may not be withdrawn before the lapse of a reasonable period.

3. The death of a seller before the option to purchase has been exercised by the buyer can entail very considerable problems. It must be remembered that there is nothing equivalent to the English Executor and it is all the heirs individually of the deceased seller who stand in his shoes. If one heir is not *sui juris* for reasons of age or capacity, interminable delays can occur.

4. The option given to the buyer must be exercised most strictly in accordance with the provisions in the contract or it will be ineffective and the option lost.

5. It must be noted that a purchaser under such a contract has until actual exercise of his option very limited rights and cannot extend these by registration or otherwise. Thus he has no rights as against mortgagees in any action taken by them to foreclose or exercise rights of sale even if the contract were entered into prior to the commencement of such action. In the bankruptcy of the seller, his rights are merely those of one of a number of unsecured creditors.

6. As the law stands at present, the rights of a buyer in a case where the seller disregards the option he has given and sells elsewhere are against the seller in damages only, notwithstanding the registration of the contract at the Land Registry, but if a buyer completes the purchase of property with the

knowledge of the existence of a prior *promesse de vente*, he is jointly liable with the seller for damages. It is possible to have the 'wrongful' sale annulled but, in order to do this, the very difficult burden of proving the lack of bona fides on the part of the 'wrongful' buyer is thrust on the contracting buyer.

7. On the assumption that, under this type of contract, the seller behaves as he should, his property is 'blocked' until the buyer exercises or does not exercise his option. Here French law is faced with a dilemma. This type of contract is unilateral but recognizes not only the disadvantage to which the seller is put but also the advantage accruing to the buyer of having time in which to reach a decision to buy or not to buy. In England, there seem to be no such jurisprudential heartsearchings about a straightforward grant of an option in consideration of a payment of cash. French law has compromised and accepted that a purchaser may, provided it does not exceed a reasonable proportion (usually taken as ten per cent) of the purchase price, pay to the seller an amount to be taken as on account of the purchase price if the option is exercised and lost to the seller if it is not, without the contract's losing its basically unilateral character. Interestingly enough, if the contract provides for an amount to be paid by the seller as a penalty should he default in his obligations, the contract becomes automatically a bilateral *compromis de vente*.

Compromis de vente

1. Such a contract may be by either notarial or non-notarial document but it is rare in the case of a private dwelling-house for the contract to be other than s.s.p. On the other hand, such a contract comes within the provisions of Article 1589 of the Code Civil, which states that, where there is agreement as to subject matter and price, a promise to sell is equivalent to a sale. Whilst the sale itself can be effected only by *acte notarié*, it is worth remembering that many of the contracts drawn by sellers' Agents are prepared without a sight of the title deeds. It is, therefore, important to ensure that the contract contains all that it should.

2. A *compromis de vente* is liable to submission for stamp duty within a month of execution if it is of itself an unconditional agreement to sell and buy. In such a case, which is extremely rare, the contract and not the subsequent

acte de vente would be stamped. However, in the event of its containing conditions (which in the event it virtually always does, e.g. for title, freedom from charges etc., as well as frequently the Loi Scrivener conditions which are dealt with at length in Chapter 6), the period of one month counts from the date when the conditions are fulfilled; hence, the *acte de vente* is normally executed before the expiration of the statutory period and itself bears the stamp duty.

3. In the event of the death of a contracting seller, the property in question does not form part of his estate. The death or incapacity of either party does not give rise to the same problems as in the case of a *promesse de vente*.

4. It is usual to make on exchange of contracts payment of ten per cent of the sale price 'on account'. Preferably, this should be paid to the Notary, if only one is acting, or to the buyer's Notary, if two are involved. Naturally, sellers' Agents are very happy to take deposits. In cases where the deposit is large, it is sometimes possible to negotiate a bank guarantee instead of the deposit being paid away where it earns interest for no one. This is best left to the expert to negotiate: it is almost certain that foreign buyers will be refused this facility by a seller's agent.

5. The Code Civil requires that in the case of a bilateral contract there should be as many originals as there are parties and that the contract should state how many originals there are. Failure to observe this requirement does not render the contract void but deprives it of its intrinsic value as proof of its contents. The agreement contained in such a contract must then be proved by extrinsic evidence.

Apart from the Loi Scrivener condition, sale contracts will normally contain a number of other conditions precedent. These will relate to Planning laws and the like and also to the absence of or release of statutory rights of pre-emption. Such rights exist in certain cases of urban property where the local authority must be informed of the proposed sale and much more frequently in the case of country property where SAFER (*sociétés d'aménagement foncier et d'éstablissement rural*, State organizations whose task is to ensure that agricultural property is suitably utilized) has an over-riding right of pre-emption. Conditions as to the existence of easements in very general terms are also included but call for a word of warning. Since very many contracts are drawn by Estate Agents without a sight of the title documents, easements in respect of country properties can easily get overlooked. A purchaser of property in the country should insist on seeing a copy of the *acte de vente* to the seller; in fact, with such property and particularly if it is land for building, it is not desirable to place reliance on a seller's Agent and additional advice on the contents of the contract should be sought elsewhere.

It will doubtless be surprising to the English conveyancer to find that very many French contracts contain also a condition precedent that the property sold is not subject to any charge the amount of which is equal or superior to the sale price. It is, of course, the equivalent of the English provision that a sale shall be 'free of encumbrances'; the reason for its inclusion is to be found in the Chapter on Land Registration.

The contract will normally include a date for completion. The normal period between contract and completion is a little over a month but the Loi Scrivener rules must be taken into account in fixing a date, as must be the considerable delays which can occur in obtaining replies to Land Registry searches. Completion dates tend to be on an 'on or before' basis rather than a fixed date and frequently pass by without completion taking place.

A typical French contract will include the name of the Notary before whom the *acte de vente* will be signed. If only one Notary is shown, he will be the choice of the seller and a buyer should exercise his prerogative to choose his own Notary so that there are two Notaries, one acting for each party. Ideally, he should do this prior to exchange of contracts but he may insist on his own Notary at any time thereafter whatever the contract may say. Obvious practical difficulties can arise if this decision is left until the sole Notary named in the contract has proceeded far towards completion on the basis that he alone is involved in the transaction. Even the involvement of two Notaries does not always mean that the buyer's Notary will be the one who will 'receive' the *acte de vente* (see Chapter 7).

Contracts prepared by Estate Agents will always include a provision for the payment of their commission. It is essential to make certain that the wording lays that burden only on the seller, unless the transaction is in a part of France where normally the payment of commission is shared. Sometimes contracts will remind buyers that they alone are responsible for the costs of purchase but such an arrangement can be varied by agreement between the parties. Again, except in such areas where custom is otherwise, the buyer alone pays notarial fees and the disbursements attendant on a purchase, i.e. stamp duties and registration fees. A seller normally pays no notarial fees.

Great care must be taken to ascertain if one is buying in an area where it is not the seller but the buyer who pays sale commission. This will occur mainly in country areas and in the north and in parts of the south-west of France where it is still customary to entrust the sale of property not to an Estate Agent but to the Notary. Unless there are special reasons to the contrary, this practice will not normally be encountered in the south of the country. Where the Notary acts as a selling agent, his commission is considered to be part of the *frais d'acte* or *frais de notaire* and hence payable by the buyer. As in the case of conveyancing fees proper, this commission is on a scale basis and is shown in Appendix B.

Contracts for the sale and purchase of property 'on plan' (*vente en état futur d'achèvement*) call for special consideration; they are dealt with separately in Chapter 4.

The benefits of contracts for the purchase of land are normally readily assignable. Generally, if no mention is made of the unassignability of the contract, the mere payment of the purchase price and execution of the *acte de vente* by a person other than the contracting purchaser suffices, the contracting purchaser naturally remaining liable until so relieved from his obligations. Sometimes contracts in which the purchaser knows in advance that he is contracting for the benefit of another (e.g. a company yet to be incorporated) will indicate that he contracts for himself and on behalf of any other person who may be substituted for him. Occasionally assignment is forbidden.

From what has been said above, it will be appreciated that something less than the sanctity which attaches to completion dates in England exists in France. However, there will come a time when the delays of the defaulting party exceed what is acceptable. To resort to the Courts to enforce a contract would be a rare and tediously long process and is hardly considered in textbooks as a remedy: certainly it is one in which no non-French party should become involved if this can be avoided.

The equivalent of the English Notice to Complete is the *mise en demeure* which requires attendance at the Notary's office to complete the transaction. Failure by the defaulting party to attend results in a notarial certificate of non-attendance which is evidence that the party not in default may proceed appropriately.

The methods of enforcement utilized are therefore less designed to obtain compliance with the terms of a contract in the sense that specific performance will be obtained but rather to compensate one party and penalize the other in terms of money. In the case of the *promesse de vente*, reference has already been made to the payment which is frequently made to the seller by the party to whom the option to buy is given which is taken towards the price if the option is exercised but forfeit to the seller if it is not. This payment is called the *indemnité d'immobilisation*. This is generally considered sufficient protection for the seller. There are cases where the option-holder requires some form of protection. If this is accorded, there is every likelihood that the result will be to turn the contract from a unilateral into a bilateral agreement with all the results dealt with in this chapter. Certainly, if a payment is made in such circumstances by the seller, the option-holder is advised not to cash the cheque until the moment at which he becomes entitled to retain the sum in question.

In the case of bilateral contracts, there are three different types of payment to deal with failures to complete which may be made under or provided for in such a contract. They are:

1. *Les arrhes*. This is a deposit which by virtue of Article 1590 of the Code Civil is forfeit by the giver and returnable in double its amount by its recipient. The result is that by the mere loss or repayment of the deposit in this way, the contract is avoided so that a contract under which *arrhes* are paid is considered to be a conditional contract. For this reason, such a deposit is seldom paid under the ordinary *compromis de vente* since the parties consider themselves fully bound. Moreover,

there is the problem that, if such a deposit is too high, it will be considered by the Court to be paid not as *arrhes* but on account of the sale price, and the Court has an inherent power to consider if the loss or repayment of *arrhes* is just and equitable in all the circumstances.

2. *Le dédit.* This is a sum agreed between the parties to be paid by one party to another in the event of his failure to complete. It is to be distinguished from a penalty in that a penalty is an amount calculated to ensure compliance with the contract whilst a *dédit* is an amount on payment of which the payer may withdraw from the contract. It differs from *arrhes* in that (a) the contract may require its payment by one party only and (b) it need not actually be paid on execution of the contract (and frequently is not) but may simply be fixed in amount and its payment provided for in the contract. A defaulting party on whom a *mise en demeure* has been served who still fails to complete become liable to pay the *dédit*. It must, however, be realized that the traditional payment made on exchange of contracts is usually a payment on account of the price and not by way of *dédit*, so that the situation is not the same as the forfeiture of a deposit in England. Moreover, there are obvious difficulties when a contract is subject to the Loi Scrivener condition if the purchaser is seeking a loan. Be that as it may, very many contracts for the sale and purchase of dwelling-houses contain a *dédit* clause, and it is generally considered a reasonable and standard protection for both parties.

3. *La clause pénale.* Such a clause, intended originally to be *in terrorem* and beyond the interference of the Courts, is unlikely to be met with in ordinary house-purchase transactions. For some years now, the Court has had power to reduce (and increase) penalty clauses and to vary them in the light of the part performance of contracts. It is not permitted for parties to contract out of these provisions.

A recent innovation is the introduction of the *Assurance Automatique Acquéreur* offered by Notaries free of cost to purchasers. Under this cover, a purchaser who has entered into a contract to buy property is insured in the amount of the purchase price up to one million francs in the event of his death or accidental total disability arising before completion. The conditions of such cover becoming automatically and without any medical examination or enquiry available to a purchaser are (i) that the contract must have been signed before a Notary (thus the standard Estate Agents' contracts do not attract this benefit), (ii) the property can be houses, flats or land, leases, goodwill of a business or shares in a property-owning company, (iii) the contract must be registered or must be accompanied by a payment to a Notary of a deposit of at least 5% of the purchase price, and (iv) purchasers must not be aged more than sixty-five. The beneficiary of the policy moneys may be the purchaser(s) or their successors in title or any other person named in the contract.

4 Purchases of Property 'On Plan'

Article 1601 is the only Article contained in the Code Civil under the Heading 'Sales of property to be built'. It defines two distinct types of such sales. One is a sale evidenced by a contract under which the seller undertakes to build an edifice on land by a fixed completion date and the purchaser agrees to pay the contract price for the land and building on its completion. Such an arrangement is a sale *'à terme'*. The transfer of the property in the land is by way of the notarial *acte* attesting completion of the building work, the transfer taking effect retrospectively to the date of the contract.

The second type of sale envisaged by the Article is the sale *'en l'état futur d'achèvement'* or 'on plan'. Under such a contract the seller transfers to the purchaser all his interest in the land together with the building on it in its then present state of construction. Future additions to the building are added to the property of the purchaser as and when they come into existence, he making stage payments at defined intervals until the building works are complete.

The difference between the two types of sale is clear and does not permit a *'vente en l'état futur d'achèvement'* to be translated as 'a sale for possession on completion' as appears from time to time in translations and dictionaries. Two Statutory Instruments, No.78-621 of 31 May 1978 and No.78-622 of 31 May 1978, provide a code of sales of both types. Since the former type will rarely be met with, this chapter deals only with the latter, which is relatively common.

If, as is often the case, there is a preliminary contract, it must be in writing and a copy must be given to the intending purchaser before he makes any payment thereunder. Such a contract, which is of course bilateral, is called a *contrat de réservation* or *contrat préliminaire*. The contract must comply with certain requirements, of which the most important are the following:

1. It must contain a full description of the property to be sold, including, if it forms part of a building, its situation therein, its approximate area and number of rooms. The nature and quality of the works to be carried out must be indicated and this may be by outline specifications (*note technique sommaire*) which should include the domestic services to be provided and, if the property forms part of a larger property, the collective services such as heating.

2. The price must be stated and how stage payments are to be made and, if there are provisions for price revision, what these provisions are. Basically, the law ties revisions to one or two indices of which the Cost of Construction Index is the more popular.

3. It may not provide for the payment of a *réservation* which exceeds five per cent of the proposed sale price if completion of the sale will take place within a year or two per cent if the building will not be completed for two years; and no payment at all may be taken if completion will exceed two years. All *réservations* must be placed to the credit of a special account opened in the name of the intending purchaser at a bank or similar specially authorized institution or with a Notary.

4. It must contain in full the provisions of the paragraphs of the Statutory Instrument No.78-622 relating to repayment of the *réservation*, which state that it must (if requested) be repaid in full to the intending purchaser if

(i) execution of the *acte de vente* does not take place on the date provided for in the preliminary contract due to the default of the vendor or

(ii) the final price exceeds by more than five per cent the price in the preliminary contract even if that contract provides for a lawful variation of the price. This provision holds good even if the reason for the increase in price is an increase in the area of the property to be sold or in the quality of the specified works or

(iii) any intended loan referred to in the preliminary contract (see Chapter 6) is not obtained or can be obtained only in an amount more than ten per cent less than was shown in that contract or

(iv) the building or part of the building to be bought is to be reduced in area or in quality to an extent that its value would be reduced by more than ten per cent of the original price or if it is proposed to omit the installation of one or more of the domestic services.

Repayment of such *réservation* must be asked for by registered AR letter and, if properly repayable, must be made within three months of that demand.

5. It must also quote the paragraph of the Statutory Instrument requiring that the intending purchaser must receive a draft of the *acte de vente* at least one month prior to the date fixed for its execution.

6. It must contain full details of what guarantees against the vendor's failure to complete the building have been provided so that the purchaser may know how he will be reimbursed for stage payments made to no good end. It must also indicate the purchaser's recognition that he has been made aware of these facts. Information of this kind sometimes needs careful checking.

7. In accordance with s.20 of Law 89-1010 which has now come into force, any contact s.s.p. for a purchase 'on plan' does not become effective until 7 days after receipt by the buyer, provided he is a 'non-professional' buyer, of his part of the contract sent to him by registered AR post. This 'cooling off' period applies if the law provides for no other longer period such as the Loi Scrivener condition (see Chapter 6). Since that Law does not apply to this type of contract, it seems that there is likely to be no other such longer period applicable to a *contrat de réservation*. Notice by the buyer to cancel such a contract must be sent by registered AR post within the time limit.

Stage payments are made against architects' certificates. The basic stage payments may not exceed thirty-five per cent of the price on completion of the foundations, seventy per cent of the price when the building is made watertight, and ninety-five per cent on completion. This allows for intermediate stage payments, which are commonly taken, so long as the statutory proportion is not at any time exceeded. It will be noticed that there is a five per cent retention to which reference is made hereafter.

The *acte de vente* executed on completion must contain certain information, much of which will, or should, be a repetition of any preliminary contract. It must, in addition to fully describing the property sold and indicating its price, give the times when stage payments must be made, cover any permitted variations in the price, either give information as to the guarantee obtained by the vendor to cover failure to complete the building or make provision for the repayment of such of the purchase price as has been paid in such an event, and, if necessary by reference to documents held by a Notary, give building specifications and similar information. In the case of the purchase of property which is *en copropriété*, the *règlement de copropriété*, of which a copy should previously have been made available to him, must be handed to a purchaser.

Building is deemed to have been completed when all works and all domestic services indispensable for its occupation in accordance with its permitted user have been completed and installed. Minor deviations from the specifications or bad workmanship which is not of a substantial character and do not prevent the normal occupation of the building are not to be treated as a failure to have completed building. However, the mere acceptance that building work has been completed, at which time a balance of cash will be due, leaving only the five per cent retention, does not imply agreement on the part of a purchaser that the terms of the contract have been complied with nor do they constitute a waiver of his right in respect thereof.

These rights are contained in Article 1642-1 of the Code Civil, which states that, 'The seller ... cannot, whether before completion of [building] works or during a period of one month from the day upon which the purchaser takes possession, be relieved of liability for building faults apparent at that time. Provided that the vendor undertakes to repair such faults, the purchaser shall not be entitled to repudiate the contract or claim any reduction in the price.' These rights are in addition to the standard rights against a builder for defects which run for two or ten years depending on the nature of the defects. The withholding of five per cent of the purchase price if, on completion of the building, all seems not to be in order can therefore become of importance, especially since most developments are largely financed by banks and other similar institutions who will start asking questions if too many such amounts are withheld.

Even in cases of purchases 'on plan', the French purchaser seems reluctant to instruct any expert to inspect the building and see whether it has been built in conformity with specifications and determine the quality of the workmanship.

As is apparent in Chapter 11, in the case of a flat owned *en copropriété*, the *syndic* is responsible for the common parts of the building but each owner is responsible for his own flat. It is virtually a certainty that no block of flats has been built or will hereafter be built where the developer has not and will not be guilty of some building default and some of them can be very serious. It is standard practice for *syndics* to be waging battles against developers for at least five years after completion of the building of a block and often for a longer period. There is no reason to suppose that defects are limited to the common parts of a block. Whatever may be the views of purchasers of other nationalities, it is essential that the British cling to their tradition that the services of a surveyor or architect are necessary and no clearance to a developer or builder should ever be given by a purchaser without the benefit of such professional advice.

Generally and notwithstanding that by law moneys paid under a preliminary contract for a purchase *en l'état futur d'achèvement* should be recoverable without difficulty if things go wrong, it is even more desirable that an intending purchaser should obtain advice when contemplating such a purchase than in the case of the purchase of an existing property. On a purely practical basis, it is axiomatic that no building is completed on due date and delays can be substantial. No *contrat préliminaire* will fail to contain the most comprehensive 'get out' clauses to cover failures of this kind and buyers should assume that very many months delay may be needed before they can successfully recover damages or rescind the contract for delay on the part of the developer.

A number of developers both French and non-French are using the *contrat préliminaire* as a method of testing the market or creating an interest among potential sources of financial backing often before they have obtained any planning consents. There is nothing in law which prevents such a contract dealing with a merely projected development but it seems clear that its contents must comply with the requirements of the Statutory Instruments referred to above.

Failure to do so renders the contract void and since these requirements are *d'ordre public* and the only contract which can be executed in respect of such a transaction is one which complies with them, it is doubtful whether 'preliminary' *contrats préliminaires* such as option agreements drawn under English or the law of some other country are valid. At all events, great care must be taken when a buyer is asked to sign a contract in respect of property for which, for example, planning permission is said not yet to have been obtained or which does not wholly conform with the letter of the law. If he is asked to pay a deposit under such an agreement, even more care is called for.

Purchasers of land intending to have built an individual house to their design upon it as opposed to buying a house 'on plan' are given by the new law of 19 December 1990 important new protection and after 1 December 1991 when it comes into force, building contracts should be considered in the light of this law.

5 Powers of Attorney

Articles 1984 to 2010 of the Code Civil deal with the *Mandat* or *Procuration*. There is nothing equivalent in France to the short Power of Attorney under the Powers of Attorney Act 1971 nor to the Enduring Power. Any party to an *acte authentique* may avoid the need to be present at its execution before a Notary by appointing an Attorney in his place and any non-notarial document may also be executed by an Attorney. The *mandant* may appoint a *mandataire* either by *acte s.s.p.* or by *acte authentique* or even verbally. It is generally considered that in the case of a non-French buyer or seller of land the Power should preferably be by *acte authentique* since in this way the signature of the donor is authenticated; it must be remembered that the execution of French documents requires no attesting witness. Hence, such a document if executed in England must be executed either before a French Consul who has the powers of a Notary and is not a merely Consular Agent or before a Notary Public. To be valid in France, if it is executed before a Notary Public, the Hague Convention Apostille must be affixed. If executed in France, it will be executed before a Notary.

A Power of Attorney which authorizes certain types of transactions e.g. the taking up of a mortgage must by *acte authentique* so that a Power to purchase property where the donor is obtaining a loan or for a purchase of property still in the course of construction must in any event be in that form.

A Power to buy or sell must be in express terms and must include a reasonably full description of the property in question and the method of payment of the price in the case of a purchase and express authority to receive the price in the case of a sale. Such express powers can be include in a General Power but it would be unusual and for practical reasons not to be recommended for an English donor. As an example of

41

how precise one must be, it has been held that authority to sell a piece of land without any description as to its use will not authorize the sale of that land specifically for building purposes since the fiscal implications may differ dependent upon the use to which the land is to be put by the buyer.

It seems unlikely that in normal circumstances a *Procuration* given by an English donor will run into revocation problems but it may be useful to know that the Code Civil provides for revocation in the following circumstances:

(i) by specific revocation by the donor at any time and in any manner but the obligation to prove that the *mandataire* had notice of revocation falls on the donor.

(ii) by notice of the appointment of a new *mandataire* 'in the same matter' as a previously appointed *mandataire*. This counts as notice of revocation from the date of notification to the firstly appointed Attorney.

(iii) by the death or incapacity of the *mandant* or *mandataire*, but acts done by a *mandataire* in ignorance of the death or incapacity of his *mandant* are validly done.

The Code Civil provides (Article 2004) that the donor of a Power of Attorney may revoke it at any time. However, nothing prevents the donor from opting out of the Article, and a Power may be granted in terms that it is irrevocable for a period of time. Such a Power may nevertheless be revoked at any time if the donee has committed a breach of his duties as Attorney.

There are considerable advantages in any non-French buyer or seller of land appointing an Attorney to act for him in the transaction. As is explained elsewhere, completion dates in France tend in practice to be on the 'on or before' basis rather than a fixed date and frequently take place later than expected. Hence, for a buyer or seller to travel to France specially to execute an *acte de vente* will cost him not only his (and possibly his spouse's) fare but also probably more than one night in an hotel and considerable irritation. The cost of the preparation of a *Procuration* and of its execution is trivial in comparison with such an expense. By implication, the appointment of a suitable Attorney means that the donor has yielded conduct of the matter into the hands of someone more qualified than he, which is seldom a bad thing.

Great care must, however, be taken both with the choice of *mandataire* and with the terms of the Power itself. For all the professional responsibility which a Notary incurs in connection with Powers of Attorney, both as to their execution and as to the scrupulous performance by an Attorney of his duties, it is unfortunate that it is far from unknown for this document to arrive for execution in the form of a printed or photocopied document with blanks and often without any word of explanation as to its contents or how it should be executed. As is pointed out elsewhere, a purchaser who does not make use of his own independent adviser to deal with the Notary but tries to do so himself is unlikely to receive or, if he does receive it, to understand much advice on the impact of French law. In effect, therefore, his *Procuration* represents a useful method of giving instructions to the Notary, since this document should contain references to (a) the *état civil* of the *mandant*, including his *régime matrimonial*, or in the case of an Englishman, rather his lack of it, (b) the manner in which joint purchasers buy (see Chapter 9) and (c) how the purchase price will be paid. For this reason, either the *Procuration* should be prepared from full instructions following on full advice by someone in France with a knowledge of both French and English law or it should at least be vetted by such a person. Certain Notaries Public in England who have a knowledge of French law can deal with this problem admirably.

When Notaries do prepare Powers of Attorney and the Attorney ultimately named is not chosen by the English donor, it is common practice for the Attorney to turn out to be one of the Notary's clerks. The dangers inherent in this practice are not always apparent but can sometimes be serious. An Attorney is the *alter ego* of his donor and his duties towards his donor are both different from and more profound than those of the Notary involved in the transaction for which the Attorney was appointed. A Notary may genuinely be unaware of certain terms of a transaction and may, in certain circumstances, be allowed his ignorance. An Attorney should not be ignorant of any matter which affects how he behaves on behalf of his donor and it is submitted that it is unfair to both Attorney and donor to appoint an employee of the acting Notary and burden him with a more onerous duty than may be imposed on his employer. There are quite a number of Notaries in France who share this view but some clearly do not. The reason for this is clear. What may be safe (even if undesirable) for a French party to a transaction will not necessarily be safe or desirable for a non-French party but it is arguable that it is outside the scope of the Notary's duty to take such a view.

In cases where a purchase or sale of French property is to or by a UK company, it would not usually be advisable to have resort to Section 38 of the Companies Act 1985 and try to operate in France under an English type Power of Attorney. The best procedure is that referred to in Chapter 10.

There is no rule in France as to how long a Power of Attorney remains in force; equally there is nothing equivalent to the Statutory Declaration of non-revocation. In very general terms, many Notaries will not or at least prefer not to accept a Power which is more than (say) three months old but naturally this depends on all the surrounding circumstances. In some cases, all that is asked for is a letter of confirmation from the Donor that the Power is still in force; in others, a new Power is asked for.

Precedents for Power of Attorney to buy and sell and to deal with the estate of a deceased person are contained in Appendix A.

6 Mortgage Finance

There is, in France, no equivalent of the concept of the English Building Society but this does not mean that there is any lack of institutions whose business is that of providing house-purchase loans. Most banks will provide loans for this purpose, including the 'British' banks. As will be seen from what is said hereafter, it pays to enquire in advance even of finding a property what their current lending policy may be. In general terms, it may well take longer to obtain the offer of a loan than it does in England.

Where a simultaneous purchase and borrowing take place, there is no separate mortgage document. What would normally be contained in an English mortgage deed forms part of the *acte de vente*, the lender not being strictly a party to that document but 'intervening' in respect of the loan. It is customary for the lender to instruct the purchaser's Notary to act for him. This does not result in a reduction of fees payable by a purchaser/mortgagor, as might be the case in England, nor is there relief from Land Registry fees on a contemporaneous purchase and mortgage. On repayment of a loan, the cost of obtaining and registering a release (*mainlevée*) at the Land Registry is disproportionately high, and there is nothing equivalent to the standard undertaking to produce a Form 53. All registrations of charges automatically lapses two years after their due date of repayment. It is, therefore, common for a mortgagor who has repaid his loan other than on a sale of the property to leave the charge on the register after repayment and let it vacate itself at no charge to himself. Of course, if he sells within the two-year period, his purchaser will require a formal release on completion.

In 1979 the French Parliament enacted a Law designed to protect purchasers of property buying with the aid of a loan.

In accordance with common French practice, this Law is known as '*la Loi du 13 juillet 1979*' (the date of its enactment) or '*la Loi Scrivener*' (the name of the Minister responsible for its passage through Parliament). Its provisions are *d'ordre public*.

The Loi Scrivener protects the potential borrower in two ways. It provides, on the one hand, rules for the procedure to be followed as between lender and borrower and, on the other hand, where a purchase is to take place with the aid of a loan, it requires that the contract be made subject to the condition precedent of the obtaining of the loan. In practice, the very strict requirements as between purchaser/borrower and vendor do not seem to cause many problems but the following basic principles should be noted:

1. The Law applies only to purchases of private dwelling-houses or of property intended, as is not uncommon in France, for a mixed private and professional user. It applies also to the purchase of land for the construction of buildings intended to have such users.
2. The Law does not apply to purchases *en l'état futur d'achèvement*. There is, of course, no reason why a condition similar to that imported by the Law should not be written in a *contrat préliminaire* but it is not automatically available (see page 35).
3. It applies only to loans from 'professional' lenders, i.e. banks, lending institutions or individuals carrying on the business of making loans for property purchases. There is some doubt whether the Law applies where the whole or a part of the sale price is paid to the vendor by instalments over a period of time on the grounds that, even if the vendor is secured by a mortgage on the property sold, such an arrangement is not a loan but merely an arrangement designed to 'facilitate' payment of the price. Certainly, it would not be safe to rely on the non-application of the Law in, for example, the not altogether uncommon case of the sale of *completed* flats in a new block by a developer who is prepared to take sale prices by instalments. It is best to assume that the Law will apply in every case and to seek advice locally if a vendor attempts to argue otherwise.

4. Every purchase contract subject to the Law must contain either:

(i) reference to the fact that the purchase is made without recourse to a loan and *in the handwriting of the purchaser* a form of wording by which the purchaser recognizes that he has been informed that if thereafter he needs recourse to a loan he cannot avail himself *vis à vis* the vendor of the protection of the Law or

(ii) a statement that the purchase is being made with the aid of a loan.

5. In cases where a contract states that the purchaser will have recourse to a loan, the contract becomes automatically subject to the condition that such a loan is obtained by the purchaser. The period during which the condition remains in force may not be less than one month but may by agreement between the parties be longer. The period runs from the date of signature of the contract. The vast majority of contracts are not notarial documents the date of execution of which cannot be in question. In practice, many Estate Agents do not get the parties to sign contracts at the same time and in these cases a purchaser must be very careful, should he be the first to sign, to make certain that the contract does not subsequently get itself antedated – to, of course, the advantage of the vendor.

6. The relevant provision of the Law is somewhat laconic. It says merely that, where a loan is involved, a contract is subject to the obtaining of the loan. Article 1178 of the Code Civil states that, 'A condition [to which a contract is subject] is deemed to be fulfilled when the debtor bound by such a condition has prevented the fulfilment thereof.' The French Courts have not unnaturally applied the reasoning of this Article to rule that, if the purchaser himself through his own fault fails to obtain his loan, the condition is deemed fulfilled. More strangely, the Article appears also to have been applied to the situation of a purchaser failing to get his loan through some act of the vendor; it is said that the condition is also deemed to have been fulfilled and presumably the unfortunate purchaser will be bound to complete a purchase without a loan. One assumes that such a situation will seldom, if ever, arise. In any event, it is essential that the

condition in the contract be quite explicit in its terms, and ideally it should refer to a loan which has already been offered and the terms of which are acceptable to the purchaser/borrower and are quoted.

As between lender and borrower, the Law lays down a certain number of requirements concerning the offer of a loan and its acceptance. Of these, the most important are:

1. Every offer of a loan must be in writing addressed to the borrower. It must contain full details of the proposed loan, terms of its repayment and of its availability, the total cost of the loan including interest and any other sums payable, precise details of the interest chargeable (particularly if it is variable or subject to indexation), what, if any, ancillary assurances are required to be taken out and a statement that the offer must remain in force for thirty days.

2. The borrower may not accept the offer before the expiration of a 'cooling-off' period of ten days. Before such acceptance, which must be in writing, no money may pass either way.

3. An acceptance of a loan by a borrower is subject to the condition that the contract entered into by the borrower (i.e. the purchase contract) is completed within four months of such acceptance.

4. A borrower may at any time make early repayment in part or in whole of his loan, but the loan offer may forbid such repayment of amounts which are not in excess of ten per cent of the principal sum borrowed. The offer may require that a premium for early repayment be charged but it may not exceed an amount calculated according to the relevant Statutory Instrument for the time being in force.

5. If a borrower makes default in his repayments and the lender does not call in the loan which, of course, he will be entitled to do, he may merely increase the rate of interest within the limits fixed from time to time by Statutory Instrument until such time as the borrower has made up his default. In general terms, a borrower may always apply to the Court for relief, particularly if he becomes unemployed or is made redundant.

From a practical point of view, the 'cooling-off' period of ten days can prove a nuisance for the English purchaser/ borrower because ideally one wants to receive it just before contracts are signed but not necessarily to stay in France until the period is over. If, as is frequently advisable, the purchaser acts through an Attorney, it is useful to include in the Power of Attorney the power to deal with mortgage loans so that the offer can be taken up by an Attorney.

Virtually every loan granted in France will require the borrower to effect straight life-cover in some form or another. This requirement and its cost must be referred to in the loan offer. Sometimes medicals are required but frequently they are not.

Notaries do not normally seek or negotiate loans.

Until such time as it may become common form to borrow in one's own country on the security of property in another (a procedure which is nevertheless becoming more and more acceptable), it is generally advisable to enlist suitable assistance when seeking a house-purchase loan in France. What each lender requires as evidence of a non-French borrower's ability to service a loan varies very much from lender to lender. Those not used to non-French ways may ask for all sorts of information which the French expect to and find easy to provide (including on occasions tax returns and receipts) but usually a fairly official piece of paper certifying the applicant's income will suffice, particularly if the piece of paper emanates from a bank or firm of accountants or is in the shape of company or business accounts. Although French lenders are as intelligent as lenders in any other country, they do have a reverence for stamps, seals and signatures which perhaps the English do not. It should not be overlooked that one method of raising finance for the purchase of property in France is to obtain a bank guarantee in the UK and offer this as security for a loan in France.

As to the remedies open to a French mortgagee in the event of non-repayment, in essence they do not differ from those available in England although they are perhaps less complex in concept but slower in execution. Eventually, a defaulting mortgagor will find himself faced with a *vente judiciaire* which has the only attraction of being an auction sale conducted by the local Court in the form of a 'candle auction' at which only members of the Bar may bid on behalf of their clients. What, however, is important to remember is that, if a borrower has trouble with his French lender, he should always communicate with him by registered AR post and that it is desirable to confirm any verbal arrangement in the same manner. Even if the written word is not wholly sacrosanct in France, lack of the written word can come close to proof of the non-existence of agreements made by word of mouth.

7 Towards, On and After Completion

A usual period between exchange of contracts and completion provided for in a contract is about five weeks. Suffice it to say that there seems to be lack of urgency or ability to keep to a pre-fixed date to an extent which would not be acceptable in England and to make it quite pointless for the Notary or Notaries involved on being instructed to make a diary entry of the contract date for completion.

The real problem in keeping to a contract date for completion lies in the lack of urgency evident in dealing with most matters in France which involve any branch of the law or any public office. This is ubiquitous and all-pervading. It affects every step which must be taken leading to completion of a sale. As a result, it is impossible even for the most experienced to say with any degree of certainty when anything will happen, be it the return of Land Registry Search, the answer to any question raised with the tax authorities or the arrival of a document or even mortgage moneys from some office. This does not mean that completion never takes place on due date: infrequently it does. It is, however, seldom wise for an English buyer or seller to plan in advance a visit to France to execute the *acte de vente* on the date fixed in the contract without accepting the risk that the journey may be fruitless or expensively extended. No journey should be organized until the date of actual completion has been confirmed.

Fiscal matters generally are outside the scope of this book but reference must be made to the Capital Gains Tax (CGT) situation on the sale of French land owned by persons not fiscally domiciled in France. In the event of any such tax being payable on a sale, it will be paid by the Notary out of the proceeds of sale.

There has for a number of years been an exemption from

CGT for French citizens residing abroad on the sale of one (but only one) property owned by them in France as their residence in that country since such property could not enjoy the principal private residence exemption. In 1988, the Nice Administrative Court held that this exemption applied to a Belgian owner of French property on the grounds that the Franco-Belgian tax treaty contained provisions for reciprocal fiscal benefits to be available to the citizens of both countries. Either by design or by oversight (it must be assumed by the former), the French Revenue chose not to apply this ruling. In 1989, a question was put to the Finance Minister in the French Parliament asking what steps he intended to take since many foreigners were 'fraudently' seeking French nationality in order to obtain this exemption which was available only to French nationals. The answer was that the Minister intended thenceforward to apply this exemption to all EEC nationals and to nationals of other countries which had suitable tax treaties with France. Such exemption, as for French citizens, can be claimed once only and only if the property is available for the occupation of the owner; hence no property bought for letting will qualify.

The general rule in respect of French CGT is that any person who is not fiscally domiciled in France is required on the sale by him of property in that country to appoint an *agent fiscal accredité* who is responsible for an ensuing period of four years for any such tax found due over and above that paid on the occasion of the sale. Such an agent is normally a French bank which if appointed will frequently, in addition to charging a fee, require the retention of part of the proceeds of sale if alternative security to cover its liability is not provided.

It is, however, possible to obtain a *dispense* from the appointment of an *agent fiscal accredité* if application is made *prior* to completion on the appropriate form accompanied by a copy of the agreed *acte de vente*. A *dispense* will normally be granted if either on the face of it there is no CGT payable or if the amount of such tax can be agreed and the French Revenue is satisfied that it will have no reason to reopen the file. It is essential to remember that notwithstanding that the proceeds of a sale may be exempt on the grounds referred to above, it is still necessary to obtain a *dispense* prior to completion and no seller should complete until he has satisfied himself that such a *dispense* has been obtained by the Notary acting for him.

It is regrettable that, as at mid-1990, the French tax authorities, whilst conceding that this exemption applies to the appropriate non-French citizens, are 'systematically rejecting' all applications for a *dispense* on these grounds. The reason given is that there is not sufficient staff available to check whether the conditions of the exemption have been fulfilled and therefore it is safer to refuse the application. The iniquity is that once an application has been made on the grounds that the sale is exempt from CGT and refused, it is not possible to lodge another application on the grounds that no CGT is payable or that its amount can readily be established. Great care must therefore be taken in this matter until, if at all, the French tax authorities reform.

It is by no means unknown for the application – on whatever grounds – to be overlooked and a *dispense* cannot be granted after completion. Since the agreed *acte de vente* must accompany the application and in some cases it may not be possible for the seller's Notary to lodge this in time to receive the *dispense* before completion, this is another reason for the uncertainty in completion dates.

There are other exemptions available both to French and non-French owners and sellers should obtain advice in respect of these from suitable sources.

The use of a suitably experienced Attorney resident in France is recommended. Mention has been made in Chapter 5 of the need for care in the choice of a suitable Attorney, and this is indeed by no means always an easy choice to make. All other considerations apart, the choice of Attorney falls best on someone who can be trusted to exert pressure in the interest of his donor, including the obtaining for a seller the *dispense* for CGT, which usually means someone outside the office of the Notary involved.

It must be remembered that at least in the case of town properties, where admittedly there is possibly less to go wrong than with country properties the average French buyer seems much less interested in the technique of becoming the owner of a new house or flat than does the typical English buyer. It may be that the use of one Notary to act effectively for both seller and buyer has engendered an attitude akin to that created by the US system of title insurance. Whatever the reason may be, no French purchaser would expect progress reports from the Notary leading up to completion and in general terms he arrives at completion in total ignorance of any of the legal (but not of the practical) issues involved in his purchase. The extent to which these are discussed at completion, when it is the function of the Notary receiving the *acte de vente* to ensure that both parties know what they are doing and that what they are doing represents what they intended to do, depends, it must be assumed, on how intelligent the Notary judges those attending before him to be. The point is that typical correspondence passing between a Notary and a buyer or seller, be he French or not, will be almost entirely bereft of explanations and limited to ascertaining if the parties will attend in person or by Attorney and, in the case of a buyer, advising what the costs and disbursements will amount to. An English buyer or seller must be prepared for this. Unless he has an adviser of his own, he must raise questions with the Notary prior to completion and not expect the Notary to seek to advise him on a wide variety of matters without prompting.

As is explained in Chapter 11, it will be very rare that a buyer is not deemed to have constructive notice of the contents of the *réglement de copropriété* governing the flat he is buying. It must not be assumed that, as would be the case in England such an important document will be disclosed to a buyer prior to exchange of contracts. It is comparatively rare for this document to be in evidence even at completion or for its import explained by the Notary to the buyer. Service Charge accounts are infrequently available for inspection and at best a seller will disclose a figure which it is not always easy to check. The only correct advice which can be given in this respect is that the *réglement de copropriété* and the Service Charge accounts should be inspected before any contract is signed and that the seller's agent be asked to obtain these.

Frequently, it will be one of the Notary's Managing Clerks who goes through the *acte* with the Notary appearing at the last moment for actual signature or even signing it after the parties have left. This is standard and wholly acceptable practice and represents no particular hazard where the parties are all French or where a foreign party is represented by an Attorney versed in French conveyancing practice and that of the foreign party's country. It may be less satisfactory if one of the parties is foreign and non-French-speaking and unversed in the law of his own country. Special arrangements can be made within a Notary's office for *actes* to be signed in his absence, since prima facie it is his presence which confers authenticity upon a document and clearly he cannot be both in and out of the office at the same time or attending the signature of more than one document.

As to the provision of funds from outside France to meet the payment due at completion, it is worthwhile remembering that banking is not always particularly swift in France. On the whole, it is desirable for a purchaser to open a bank account in France to receive cash from abroad and transfers from the UK direct to Notaries should not be made if any other method is available. This is no reflection on the profession but merely on the time which, having regard to the special banking arrangements required to be made by Notaries, such transfers can take.

Every *acte de vente* contains an 'affirmation of sincerity' which relates to the consideration stated in the document. In theory, the Notary is supposed to have warned the parties of the sanctions which may be exacted if the sale price is incorrectly shown either because it is understated or for any other reason. Among the reactions available to the tax authorities to a clear understatement of value is the right to buy in the property at the price quoted in the *acte de vente* plus ten per cent. It is a right rarely exercised but sufficiently frequently for Notaries to notice from time to time an otherwise unexplained (though it must be admitted short-lived) increase in property prices appearing in *actes de vente*. From this right of the State to exercise a right of pre-emption within a period of three months (in certain circumstances increased to six months) follows the difficulty, if not the impossibility, of re-selling property within that period from the date of registration at the local *Bureau des Hypothèques*.

It is, in this connection, necessary to refer to what can only be accepted as the well-established habit of parties to a sale to understate the sale price in the *acte de vente* and to settle the difference in cash. It is self-evident that, since it is fraudulent, no adviser should associate himself with such a practice. The problem is that it exists and it is not unusual to be faced with a situation where the parties to a sale have already entered into a contract which assumes by its terms an additional cash payment. Indeed, it is not by any means unknown for a transaction to stand or fall by whether one of the parties is willing to indulge the other party in this way or not.

The dangers are obvious. In the first place, there is the State's right of pre-emption. In the second place, an undervalued acquisition price may well needlessly create a Capital Gains Tax liability on resale unless again the same fraud is perpetrated, which even if the sale is exempt from such tax will still have to show an incorrect price if doubts are not to be sewn in the mind of the French Revenue. But even more dangerous is the fact that the contract will show too low a price and there is no means of dealing with the unrecorded balance (sometimes paid in advance) if one party reneges. It is, in fact, a not uncommon practice for Estate Agents to prepare and have signed two contracts – one at the false and one at the true price and to destroy the latter when all has been completed.

A much more insidious situation often involving an agreement to understate the price is that when Article 1674 of the Code Civil is involved. The effect of the Article is as follows. If A sells land for B for X francs and B resells that land to C for Y francs, if X francs is less than seven-twelfths of 'the market value' which prima facie is taken to be Y francs, A may at any time during a period of two years from the date of the sale by A to B require the recission of that sale. This right to rescind a sale *pour cause de lésion* cannot be waived by A either by contract or by way of gift. Any genuine increment in value such as restoration of a property or the obtaining of some planning consent is, of course, taken into account. If a claim is made against B, he may agree to reconvey the property to A or he may pay A the appropriate difference in value. The result is that if B opts for the former because he cannot find the necessary funds, C will lose his property and will be left with only a money claim against B. This problem most frequently arises on purchases from property dealers who are often also the selling agents. It must be watched carefully since in most cases the true reason for the request to the buyer to understate the price may be an attempt to hide the *lésion* right of action which will not be revealed until title is deduced. Should the situation arise, a buyer should either refuse to complete or require the seller to provide a guarantee to cover any claim by the previous seller during the rest of the statutory period.

If called on to advise on or to become involved in such transactions, it must always be remembered that apart from the special *lésion* situation referred to above they exist in part because stamp duty rates are very high and in part because it is a tradition in France (and indeed in certain other countries) to indulge on principle in tax evasion. To avoid it by refusing to advise can be in the interest of neither party and a 'holier than thou' attitude is a disservice to both. The only proper action which can be taken is to explain all the dangers and allow the parties to make their own decision coupled with a clear statement of disassociation. It is evident that such matters should not be discussed with the Notary involved since he has a direct personal obligation to the State.

Every contract will show who is the Notary who *reçoit l'acte*. Obviously, if only one Notary is involved, it will be he before whom the *acte de vente* is signed. If there is a Notary acting for the seller and another for the buyer, provided the property is within the area in which a Notary may authenticate the conveyance it is desirable that this be done by the Notary acting for the buyer and the contract should clearly so state. If the property is outside his area, completion will take place at the *étude* of the Notary within the area. Normally, in the case of developments of new buildings, completion will take place at the office of the developer's Notary. This does not mean that a Notary wherever his *étude* may be cannot deal with a land transaction anywhere in France; it is only his right to be the Notary who authenticates the *acte* which is in issue.

At completion the seller's agent will inevitably be present. Ostensibly, he is there to see that the sale he negotiated takes place. He renders his account for commission and usually gets paid immediately. This seems to be a matter entirely between the party or parties to the contract and agent and there is no moral or other obligation on the part of the Notary to see this commission paid. Strictly, an agent may not bring to completion the difference between any deposit he obtained and his commission. What he received must be accounted for in full. Indeed, most Notaries will pay agents commission only on a *bon de commission* marked by the person liable or his Attorney '*bon pour paiement*'. Normally, execution of the *acte de vente* is proof of the agent's entitlement to his commission but, of course, if the sale is 'unmade', it becomes repayable. Questions may, of course, arise if there is a cash payment in addition to the disclosed sale price.

As indicated in Chapter 11, the *syndic* of a *copropriété* in which a flat is being sold will be notified of the sale by the Notary for the seller, and he will be asked for a figure of Service Charges apportioned to the date of sale. The amount reported to the Notary by the *syndic* as due will be paid out of the proceeds of the sale against the seller's or his Attorney's '*bon pour paiement*'. The rule is that, in addition to ordinary Service Charges, an amount may be called for in respect of works previously voted to be done but not at the date of the sale carried out. This arrangement may be varied by agreement between seller and buyer (it is not binding on the *syndic*), and it must be said that enquiry into decisions of the *copropriété* of this nature seems often not to be adequately made. It is a rule that the *syndic* has a lien on *the whole* of the sale price in the hands of the Notary until payment of the amount claimed by him.

There does tend to be a somewhat longer delay than would be tolerated in the UK in the proceeds of sale becoming available to the seller. Quite apart from the need on the sale of property *en copropriété* before making any payment to settle what is due to a *syndic*, it is not unusual for the whole or such part of a purchase price as is not provided by way of loan to be paid by the purchaser's personal cheque. Clearing times in France are considerably longer than in Britain. Even Bank drafts are not treated as cash and value is not given until they are cleared as though they were an ordinary cheque. There may also be Land Registry problems which, while they do not hold up completion, may make it undesirable to pay out sale moneys. These reasons (and an apparent lack of the tradition – if not requirement – that binds Solicitors in this respect) account for delays in not always obtaining swift payment of the proceeds of sale. Suffice it, however, to say that, if it were absolutely necessary to use this morning's sale proceeds to buy a new property in the afternoon, this could with the assistance of a helpful Notary and the collaboration of a number of other persons be organized. It would be a very unusual arrangement for the French, who are not used to 'chain' transactions, and not one the success of which could be guaranteed in every part of the country.

In the case of a purchase, it will be weeks, if not months,

before the *expédition* of the *acte de vente* is available. This is due to the delays at the local Land Registry, since the *expédition* cannot be prepared until registration has been completed. There are Notaries who do not send out *expéditions* unless asked to do so, which is, for the English buyer, a practice much to be deplored. To those who are used to being advised of the availability of their title deeds, this may seem strange, but it is not serious. At best the *expédition* of an *acte authentique* is a kind of Office Copy issued by the local Land Registry. The original will always remain in his files and a note of its execution is kept in the Notary's official records. It must be remembered that the Notary is by virtue of his office a storer of documents and not therefore subject to the desire on the part of many Solicitors to dispose as quickly as possible of documents which otherwise clutter up his office. Because of the inevitable delay which will occur before any documentary evidence of his purchase is available to the buyer, should this be needed (e.g. for the duty free import of furniture), the Notary involved will always provide an *attestation d'acquisition* which will be accepted everywhere as evidence of ownership.

In the case of a sale, the lack of the *expédition* or even of an ordinary copy of the *acte de vente* under which the seller bought need cause no problem. Provided the name of the Notary who received that document and the approximate date of its execution are remembered by the seller, a copy can easily be obtained from that Notary. Strictly, on a sale, the *expédition* of the *acte de vente* executed on the purchase by the seller should be handed over to the buyer but this is a rule now much honoured in its breach. If the *expédition* is available and is not forgotten in the file, it will be handed over but no completion will fail for want of this document.

There is no system in France equivalent to the apportionment of *taxe foncière* or *taxe d'habitation* by the authority which levies them. In both cases, they are, so far as the tax authorities are concerned, due from the owner or occupier, as the case may be, as at 1 January prior to the sale. Most *actes de vente* will contain a provision that the buyer is responsible for the payment of (*inter alia*) these outgoings as from the date of completion, but they are not apportioned, as in England on a completion statement, and dealt with by adjustment of the sale price. In practice, the loss or gain usually lies where it falls.

French insurance law can hold surprises for the British

property-owner. Among these is that, as a general rule, French policies do not lapse on failure to pay the renewal premium; they continue in force, for a time and until formal notice of cancellation is served by the company, and the insured is pressed to pay the outstanding premium and ultimately sued if he does not do so. Policies will state the terms upon which a policy may be cancelled. These will require a period of notice, which will be a standard period (which under 1990 legislation cannot be longer than two months) in normal circumstances and a shorter period to cover unusual events, e.g. health or family circumstances of the insured. A sale will allow cancellation by the seller without notice.

On the other hand, the French Insurance Code provides that, on a sale, fire cover passes automatically to the buyer, in which case the buyer may either continue the cover with the possibility of its cancellation at some date in the future in accordance with the terms of the policy or of cancelling it on the sale but then subject to such penalty as is provided for in the policy which may not exceed one year's premium. Such provision is not *d'ordre public* and may and frequently is (and in the case of an English buyer should be) varied in the *acte de vente* to provide for cancellation of the existing policy by the seller and for the buyer to effect his own cover. Likewise on a sale, it is safer for the policy to be cancelled and for the purchaser to effect his own cover.

As is apparent, the task of a Notary is not that of a Solicitor 'hand-holder'. It follows therefore that dealing with the insurance of houses or flats on purchases or sale is not within the scope of his duties. This may surprise the English who are used to their Solicitor arranging cover on a purchase and cancelling cover on a sale. It also may cause difficulties if a buyer is left to approach a French company or broker on his own. The covers, exclusions and procedures are very different from those prevailing in England. It is also necessary to remember that although there are 'English' companies willing to provide cover on French property, the policies written will normally be according to French law and practice. Lloyd's policies written in the UK subject to English law. Ideally, if it is not to be dealt with by a local adviser with knowledge of both French and English problems, this is a matter best left to English insurance brokers of repute who specialize in the insurance of property outside the UK.

8   Land Registration

Whilst it is not necessary for the English practitioner to be familiar with the day-to-day working of the French Land Registry system, a passing knowledge of its functions will help provide an explanation of why the system is so fundamentally different in both concept and everyday practice from the English system.

Although France has a comprehensive system of land registration in the sense that all land appears on the cadastral register of some area and all transactions in land are recorded at the *bureau des hypothèques* (the equivalent of the English District Land Registry), very little of the law or practice attaching to that system finds any counterpart in the English system. Indeed, the very object of the registration of a land transaction in France is different from the object of its registration in England. Whereas the English system of land registration is designed, as the preamble to the Land Registration Act 1925 has it, 'to give certainty to the title to real estates', no such intention motivates the French system. A decision of the Courts alone can give 'certainty of title'.

This fundamental difference becomes readily understandable when it is appreciated that the French land registration system comes under the control of the French Treasury, so that one may rightly imagine that the system was created primarily for the purposes of taxation rather than for the benefit or protection of owners of land or of interests in land and of those dealing with them.

Land registration in France comprises two separate but interlocking systems. Of these, the *Cadastre*, is the country-wide register maintained at a local level which forms the basis for the valuation of land for the purpose of the imposition of *taxe foncière*, which is a tax on the ownership of land. Established by Napoleon but progressively revised since 1930, virtually all land in France is now identifiable by reference to the updated registers (*le cadastre renové*). Each *commune*, which may vary in size from large town to small village, has its own cadastral plan, extracts from which look very much like Office Copy English Land Registry plans, save that, whilst boundaries of each *lot* are of course marked and each *lot* is numbered, there is no indication of which *lots* are included in any particular title. It is possible therefore to bespeak such a plan and, having received it, only to identify the land in issue after reference to the title deeds; they will contain a description of the land involved by reference to its geographical location (probably the *commune*) and its *lot* number or numbers. Thus, it may be very difficult to obtain this vital information at pre-contract or contract stage, if the seller or his agent is unaware of the cadastral *lot* numbers.

This lack of a plan specifically linked to a numbered title means that there is no need to remove land from a registered title on a transfer of part. This in turn means that a cadastral plan showing a large plot which has become divided may well show its original number struck through and the plot divided into a number of smaller plots with new numbers. Considerable confusion can thus be caused in country properties. If purchase contracts do refer to *lot* numbers, these will be by reference to what appears in the *acte de vente* to the seller and may take no account of what the seller has in the meanwhile sold off. It seems rare to include plans with marked boundaries in *actes de vente*. On the other hand, searches of the *Cadastre* are open to the public.

It is, of course, part of the Notary's task to ensure that the cadastral description of land in an *acte de vente* is correct and, strictly speaking, that on, say, a sale of part of the seller's land, the correct alterations to the *lot* numbers are made by the *Cadastre*. It is, however, ultimately what is contained in the *acte de vente* which provides overriding evidence of title. The cadastral registers and plans are merely administrative documents, which can only provide evidence to support (if in fact they do) the presumption of ownership which flows from the documents of title themselves. Unfortunately, the *Cadastre* abounds in errors and pre-eminently in two respects – boundaries and easements. Not without remarkable simplicity of expression, one textbook puts the situation thus: 'When what is in issue is not the ownership of property but ... simply to fix a dividing line between two properties, proof of the extent [of the properties] may take any form, since what is involved is a question of fact and not one which stems from a legal document.' It is not surprising that the French Courts give less and less significance to what is on the *Cadastre*.

Strictly speaking, it is no concern of the *Cadastre* to indicate rights of way or other easements, which, since few *actes de vente* contain plans, would in any event mean interpreting the documents creating such rights. Easements should be revealed on the search made of the *bureau des hypothèques* but this will not be available before exchange of contracts. It is not unusual, particularly in country areas, for cadastral plans to have accumulated indications of roads, wells and other useful information which may or may not currently exist or may have or not have existed for very many years or may have never existed but which have somehow crept onto the plan. As has been said elsewhere, contracts for the sale of land can be quite cavalier and unspecific in their reference to easements and certainly in the purchase of country properties great care should be taken in establishing the existence or non-existence of easements both for the benefit of the land to be bought and to which it may be subject. To some extent, the French succession system, which often leads ultimately to the splitting-up of property into small parts, leads to the creation of easements which otherwise might not exist.

The second part of the French land registration system is that maintained by the *bureaux des hypothèques*. These are based locally, each with a *conservateur*, and may be looked on as the counterparts of English District Land Registries each with a District Land Registrar. There is at least one such office in every *département* and frequently more, depending on local need, so that, for a country with approximately the same population as England and Wales but about three times their size, there seems to be a disproportionately high number of local offices. The delays at such local offices vary from what at their shortest should nearly always be considered unacceptable in England to what would appear to make the life of the French conveyancer intolerable. Land Registration fees are charmingly called 'the Land Registrar's salary', and the *bureaux des hypothèques* also comes under the aegis of the French Treasury.

Three different registers are kept. One is a proprietorship register. A second is a property register which records all transactions and events to which a piece of land is subject. A third is a property register kept for urban properties where identification is simpler by street and number than by plot reference. There is no Charges Register as such, so that on the second or third of these registers will be shown some of the matters which would find their way onto the Charges Register of a registered title in England. Thus mortgages of various kinds will be shown, as will be easements. A rather larger variety of mortgages and charges seem to get onto the register in France than one would expect, and judgment debts and *saisies immobilières* tend to be registered against land often without the knowledge of the owner. On the other hand, one cannot register many of the things (e.g. cautions or dealings by a survivor of joint owners) which need to be registered in England by reason of its considerably more sophisticated land law.

When one realizes that the system is one of the registration of land throughout France and that there are no non-registration areas, it is surprising to learn that the primary duty of the *conservateur des hypothèques* in keeping his registers up to date is to work to the principle that a purchaser shall not be able to register his rights to land if the vendor of that land has not previously registered his. Remembering, however, not only that the *Cadastre* is avowedly a fiscal register but that, as has been said, the *bureaux des hypothèques* are also administered by the Treasury, the principle is perhaps comprehensible. Whilst it is appreciated that the Land Registry in England will not deal with a document which has not been properly stamped and that to that extent it acts as a 'longstop' for stamp duty, that is not its primary objective; its primary objective is 'to give an authoritative and final examination of title'. Under the French system, registration is not designed to complete the sale of land to the purchaser; that is achieved by agreement between the parties as to the property to be sold and the price. What is achieved by registration (*publicité foncière*) is that the transaction becomes valid as between the parties to it on the one hand and third parties on the other.

However, what may come as the greatest surprise to the English practitioner and be considered to be probably the greatest defect in the French system is the French Land Registry Search (*état hypothécaire*). Not only is there no question of the result of such a Search being available in even a matter of days (weeks or months are usual) but personal searches cannot be made, nor, normally, can the results be picked up by hand or telephoned or telexed. This alone can cause problems as to completion dates. In addition, the Search gives no protection to a prospective purchaser or mortgagee; the register is not frozen but remains open to receive registrations of every kind. Priority for the registration of transactions is a matter of date of receipt by the *conservateur* of the documents lodged for registration, and a fair amount is to be found in the appropriate French textbooks on how to deal with more than one sale by one vendor of the same property.

9 Joint Ownership

French law recognizes two types of joint ownership, *en indivision* and *en tontine*. Superficially, these correspond respectively to tenancy in common and joint tenancy. Since trusts are unknown in French law, each joint owner *en indivision* has an interest akin to a pre-1925 Law of Property Act legal estate. On the other hand, French law treats ownership *en tontine* as a sort of suspended ownership by two or more persons which crystallizes in the hands of the survivor(s) retrospectively to the date of purchase at the moment of the death of the joint owner first to die. Use of the *tontine* method of joint ownership is not as frequently used by the French as it is in England as a usual method of purchase by husband and wife. It is, in fact, looked on with some dislike and distrust by the French, although it is used, for example, by religious communities to ensure the continued ownership of property within the community (it being impossible to vest such property in trustees) and sometimes for other, more ordinary reasons.

However, no joint purchase of land in France by English buyers should be envisaged without their appreciating the difference from a succession point of view between the two types of joint ownership. Ownership *en indivision* results on the death of one tenant in common in his share passing in accordance with French rules of succession. Thus, as will be seen from Chapter 18, on the death of one of two spouses owning property *en indivision*, if there are children of the marriage or possibly of previous marriages or if the deceased joint owner leaves a surviving parent, the result can be unexpected and may well be unsatisfactory for the ill-advised. On the other hand, on the death of one owner *en tontine*, his share accrues to the survivor and the rules of entrenched succession can be bypassed.

It is almost inevitable that any Notary seeing a contract for the purchase by two persons which, as would normally be the case, is silent as to the manner in which they buy, will prepare the *acte de vente* for a purchase *en indivision*. It would, in his experience, be extremely rare that they should indulge in an *en tontine* transaction. It is, therefore, unlikely that he will explain that two methods of joint ownership are available; indeed, as cannot be too often emphasized, purchasers are unlikely to meet the Notary before actual completion so that he will have little or no opportunity to give such an explanation. Hence the desirability of including in any Power of Attorney given by joint purchasers an indication of the type of joint ownership to be used and the source of funds as is suggested in the alternative Power of Attorney to buy property to be found in Appendix A.

Although it is a procedure which is seldom used, having regard to French practice, it is possible to 'sever' a *tontine* in which case the joint owners hold thereafter *en indivision* in equal shares.

It is essential to consider what has been said about the use of the *tontine* in conjunction with the contents of Chapter 19.

In the remainder of this chapter, the expression 'joint ownership' refers to ownership *en indivision*, since there is no reference in the Code Civil to ownership *en tontine*. All that can be said on ownership *en tontine* is that each owner has the right jointly to use the property during his life but that it cannot be disposed of except with the consent of all the joint owners. An indication of the nature of the interest of each joint owner is that it is considered not to be an asset over which creditors can exercise any rights nor, of course, can it be disposed of by Will.

It is interesting to note that until 1976 all the rules applying to the common form of joint ownership – *indivision* – were to be found in the Code Civil not under the sections which deal with the ownership of property but under those dealing with the rules of succession. Indeed, the framers of the Code looked askance at joint ownership of property as both politically and economically undesirable and until 1976 the Code left this type of ownership in total disorganization. The old Article 815, which was the sole Article in the Code on *indivision*, provided only that an end could always put to the joint ownership of property notwithstanding any provision or agreement to the contrary.

French rules of succession being what they are, it is inevitable that vast amounts of property are owned *en indivision* for no other reason than that they have been inherited by close members of a deceased's family. Indeed, this type of joint ownership is called *indivision forcée*. The rules governing property so owned to be found in the current Article 815 and its eighteen modern sub-sections were therefore devised to not a small extent to solve the problems of joint ownership thrust upon beneficiaries of a deceased's estate rather than those arising from an intentional joint purchase by two or more persons. The Law of 1976 which enlarged Article 815 however also provided a new Article 1873 with a multitude of sub-clauses. This Article found its way into a totally new section of the Code Civil entitled 'Agreements relating to the exercise of rights *en indivision*' and it is this Article which now deals with the effect of joint ownership by choice of parties or, as it is known, *indivision ordinaire*.

The current rules by reference to Article 1873 where no life interests in the land in question are involved are as follows:

1. By agreement in writing, which must define the undivided shares of the property in question, the co-owners can agree to keep alive the co-ownership for a period which may not initially exceed five years but which is renewable thereafter for periods not exceeding five years at a time. The agreement may provide for perpetual renewal subject to the non-service of notice to the contrary given by one of the parties by a date before the date of expiry of the current period fixed by the agreement.

2. So long as such an agreement is in force, the most profound disagreement between the parties is necessary to persuade the Court to order determination of the joint ownership.

3. Co-owners may also agree to an indeterminate period of joint ownership. In such cases, the co-ownership may be put an end to at any time by notice, save where notice to determine is given (as the Code has it) 'in bad faith or at an inopportune time'. An example of the latter would be

immediately after an acquisition *en indivision* has been made for investment purposes or a loan secured on jointly owned property has been negotiated.

4. An agreement for a fixed period becomes automatically for an indeterminate period (i) in certain circumstances, on the death of a co-owner, (ii) if an undivided share becomes vested in a person who is not one of the original co-owners or (iii) if a company becomes one of the co-owners. It is suggested by a standard French textbook that this last circumstance has been included to 'conserve the family character' of ownership *en indivision*; if this suggestion is a correct interpretation of the intentions of the legislature, the French State has not wholly been able to shed its dislike of jointly owned property evinced at the time of the passing of the Code Civil in its original terms.

Co-owners may, of course, rely *ab initio* on the provisions of Article 815 and do without an agreement. If an agreement for a fixed period is not renewed, Article 815 will thereafter govern the co-ownership. The situation then as to determination of the joint ownership will be as provided for in that Article, i.e. that no one can be compelled to remain *en indivision* unless the contrary is provided for by agreement (which will not apply) or relief from determination is granted by the Court.

The application of these rules to the average purchaser of a private dwelling-house is unlikely to cause serious problems. General management rules are usually contained in the *acte de vente* under which jointly owned property is purchased or may rarely be set out in a separate document. For the straightforward purchase of a single property, it is unlikely that a *gérant* need be appointed to manage the property. If a *gérant* is named, this can be done either at the time of purchase or at a later date. If the *gérant* is one of the co-owners, he can only be dismissed in the circumstances agreed to by all the co-owners in the regulations governing the management of the property or by a subsequent unanimous resolution of all the other co-owners. If he is not a co-owner, he may be removed by a majority in number and value of the co-owners. In the case of the removal of a *gérant* who is a co-owner, his removal results in the co-ownership becoming automatically for an indeterminate period. It is said that this is to discourage people from agreeing to buy *en indivision* only if they are appointed to manage the property.

The powers of a *gérant* may not exceed those given by Article 1873. In any event, they do not include disposing of or mortgaging the jointly owned property or granting leases except in limited measure. It follows that, if no *gérant* is appointed, no co-owner can do on his own what a *gérant* cannot do. The practical answer for English co-owners not resident in France will often be to appoint an Attorney to act for them.

An important rule is that a co-owner wishing to dispose of his share for value to a purchaser who is not another co-owner must give a month's notice of his intention to sell to his co-owners who have rights of pre-emption (in the proportions in which they own their shares) in respect of that undivided share. The rule does not, however, apply to gifts of undivided interests in land.

Except possibly in country districts, purchases from owners *en indivision* should not give rise to any special difficulties. However, in parts of France (as in other countries where Code Napoleon or similar rules of succession apply and where the conservation of property within the family plays a larger part than it does in Great Britain), the mixture of peasant mentality and the existence of large families can result in the break-up of land into very small parcels or the retention of large parcels *en indivision*. Such a situation can provide many frustrations for a would-be buyer and indeed for his Notary. When a purchase of such property is contemplated, it is essential that no contract is signed without proper prior advice.

10 Companies as Owners of Land

Realty in France, irrespective of the domicile, residence or nationality of its owner, is subject to all the incidences of French law and, in particular, to French rules of succession. French personalty devolves on the death of its owner in accordance with the laws of the country of his domicile. If there are, as indeed there may well be, disadvantages to the English owner of French land which would not exist if English law applied, can such disadvantages be avoided? One solution is to turn realty into personalty through the interposition of a company between the purchaser of the land and the land itself.

Such a solution clearly cannot apply in every case and its use calls for very careful consideration of all the aspects of a purchase of land. In certain limited cases it may be desirable to make use of a French company but more usually, for a non-French buyer, a non-French company will be a preferable medium. The more important points to bear in mind are as follows:

1. Certain non-French companies owning land in France are liable to an annual tax charged on the capital value of the land in question as at 1 January every year. For most practical purposes, the companies so penalized are those incorporated in countries which do not have a Double Tax Convention with France which includes a provision for the exchange of fiscal information. Strictly speaking, however, the tax is payable by reference to the place of a company's *siège social* and not to the country of incorporation. A list of countries (excluding a number of primarily francophone countries which it seems unlikely the average British buyer would consider suitable) which are exempt from this tax (currently standing at 3%) appears in Appendix C. A *siège social* has been defined by the Finance Law 1990 as the 'seat

of effective management'. It is, however, very unlikely that if a non-French company is chosen as the owner of property in France, its 'seat of effective management' will be outside the country of incorporation but care should be taken to see that it is not in a non-exempt country and the definition brings within the scope of the tax French companies so managed.

2. However, companies which are prima facie exempt from this tax may become liable to it if all or any of their shareholders are themselves companies which would be non-exempt if they were direct owners of land in France. The amount of the liability depends on the proportion of capital held by the non-exempt company or companies.

3. Not only are shares in a non-French company owning land in France personalty but the death of a shareholder does not involve any change of ownership of the land itself. However, the death of a shareholder owning more than fifty per cent of the issued capital of a company owning French land gives rise to a claim for French death duties in respect of an aliquot part of the value of the land.

4. Until such time, if ever, as France ratifies the Convention on the law applicable to trusts which is scheduled to the Recognition of Trusts Act 1987, French law does not recognize trusts. A nominee shareholding is therefore treated as the property of the nominee and not of the beneficial owner. It must be remembered that carelessly chosen nominees can lose the company all or part of its exemption but subject to that warning, the use of nominee shareholders can be of value.

5. It is a pre-requisite to exemption from the tax that the company in question file annually a Return showing the estimated market value of the property and the names and addresses of the shareholders. The French Revenue will normally accept market values calculated from year to year by reference to the Inflation Index used for Capital Gains Tax purposes. It is, of course, from such a Return that changes of shareholders and the proportions of shares held by each shareholder can be noted.

6. French tax law provides that every non-French company carrying on business in France is prima facie liable for Corporation Tax on the fruits of its French activities, and in addition to a small tax which is payable irrespective of whether a liability to Corporation Tax arises or not. In theory, therefore, a non-French company owning French land and not

in receipt of profits which would make it liable to Corporation Tax is liable to this *taxe forfaitaire.* In the case of (say) a UK company owning property in France, the French Revenue will assume in the absence of evidence to the contrary that it is engaged in letting the property. This will result in a charge to tax based on the rental value which is usually calculated as a percentage of the capital value of the property as disclosed in the Annual Return referred to in (5) above, less an amount for expenses. However, the practice seems to be that, if the property is occupied rent free by the Directors or shareholders of the company or even by employees of the company and the appropriate annual return is made, no charge to Corporation Tax will be raised; nor usually will the *taxe forfaitaire* be charged. The Revenue has power to require a non-French company to nominate a fiscal representative in France. The difficulty is that there appears to be no uniform Revenue practice in this respect and whatever the law may be, variations in applying it occur all over the country and in the same parts of the country from time to time.

7. The use of a non-French company as the owner of land in France can also avoid Capital Gains Tax on a non-exempt sale. The sale, particularly if to a citizen of the country in which the company is incorporated, can be by way of a sale of the shares, thus not only avoiding a change of ownership but making a very considerable saving of French Stamp Duty, which at least for the English buyer can often be surprisingly high. On many occasions such a sale of shares is by no means unattractive also to a French buyer.

Apart from the application of the above points to any particular situation, there are primary decisions to be made if a purchase is to be made in the name of a company and not in the name of a private individual. In what country is the company to be incorporated – in France or out of France?

The occasions when English purchasers, advised to purchase through the medium of a company, will find the use of a French company advantageous will clearly be rare, but occasions may arise. However, it must be remembered that the type of French company which would normally be used for such a purpose i.e. a *société civile immobilière*, whilst it is treated essentially as a legal entity of its own by French law, is much more akin to a partnership than an English company both as to the liabilities of its shareholders and from a fiscal point of view. In addition, although, if the shareholders are domiciled out of France, the shares will pass on a death in accordance with the law of the deceased shareholder's domicile and not French law, French death duties will be payable. In this connection, it must be remembered that there is no surviving spouse exemption in France and that the threshold at which death duties begin to be payable is, even in the case of beneficiaries who are close relatives, much lower than in England. Hence there may well be no advantage to be gained from the Double Tax Convention and nothing against which French death duties can be set off. Unlikely though it may be that the situation will arise, it should be remembered that the liability to the 3% tax referred to above applies since 1 January 1990 to French as well as non-French companies which have their seat of effective management in a non-exempt country.

The disappearance of the UK non-resident company and the fact that most UK companies used for the purchase of property in France will be close companies means that in many cases such companies cannot safely be used for such purposes whether the beneficial shareholders are resident for tax purposes in the UK or not. However, since England can offer the advantage of the surviving spouse exemption for Inheritance Tax purposes coupled with the fact that the cost of incorporating and running an exempt company in the UK can be low compared to that in other countries, it is worth taking careful advice on the choice of company as buyer of French land. It also seems sensible to choose a country from the Appendix C list whose company law is based on English company law or at least is comprehensible by English advisers.

From a French conveyancing point of view, the purchase of land by a non-French company should not give rise to any particular problems if there is involved on behalf of the purchasing company someone with a knowledge of the requirements of French law and of the company law of the country of incorporation. This is particularly important in the case of a country, where the administration of a company is basically different from that of a French company and the functioning of the French Companies Registry, which is locally based, differs from that in the country of incorporation. For every purchase (or sale) by a UK company, there is required (a) a certified copy of the Certificate of Incorporation (b) a certified copy of the Memorandum and Articles of Association (c) a Board Resolution authorizing a person (usually a Director) to execute on behalf of the company a French Power of Attorney and (d) a *certificat de coutume* or Affidavit of Law, in French and made preferably by a suitably qualified English lawyer, confirming the company's power to enter into the transaction. A precedent of such an Affidavit is to be found in Appendix A. If the company in question is not UK incorporated but incorporated in a country whose Company Law is based on the current or a previous English Companies Act, the precedent will need little amendment.

Both the benefits and the traps of the purchase of French land through a non-French company can be considerable. Suffice it therefore to say that it is a transaction which demands the closest co-operation between advisers competent in English and French law and probably that of a third country if the most advantageous results are to be achieved and problems avoided.

A wholly different problem is posed where land is owned by a company whose shares give the right to the ownership of a part of that land. Such companies are called *sociétés d'attribution* and the acquisition of a dwelling-house through the medium of such a company requires careful advice.

Such companies are formed usually for the purchase of land with a view to the construction of a block of flats on it. The 'company' will be a *société civile immobilière* of the kind referred to above. As has been indicated, it is not a limited liability company, and basically each shareholder is liable for that proportion of the debts of the company which his shareholding bears to the total capital of the company. In many cases this will not be as dangerous as it sounds. The cost of building will probably be guaranteed by a bank or similar institution and there should be no other liabilities but gross mismanagement of the company or fraud on the part of those managing it could entail unexpected liabilities, as, of course, could rather more mundane occurrences. There may also be difficulties in obtaining loans for the purchase of the property until such time as the shares produce, on the liquidation of the company, the full ownership of the land as opposed to the right to own the land on liquidation.

A practical problem will often be that the *société d'attribution* will, as is the case of *sociétés civiles*, be managed by a *gérant* who is almost certain to have been appointed not by the shareholders but by the developer of the property, who will also be the promoter of the company. During the life of the company, the situation as between shareholder and company is very similar to that which exists between *copropriétaire* and *copropriété*. Calls will from time to time be made to meet the costs of building, administration and management. These are not in the nature of calls on partly paid shares but resemble moneys due from shareholders in a company limited by guarantee, arising by virtue of the provisions of the company's Articles (*Statuts*).

Usually there are no provisions in the Articles which prevent the free transfer of shares should an owner wish to sell prior to liquidation. However, whilst on a sale of a flat or house the seller gives the equivalent of a covenant for title, on a sale of shares in a *société d'attribution* this covenant extends only to the shares themselves and not to the underlying property. In addition, once a transfer of shares has been approved by the company and subject to any agreement between the parties to the contrary, the transferee does not take over such liability as the transferor may have to the company at the date of transfer.

Sociétés d'attribution fall within that group of French companies known as *sociétés de transparence*, that is to say, companies which are treated for fiscal purposes as not having a legal personalty of their own separate from that of each individual shareholder. Hence a transfer of their shares is treated as a transfer of land for Capital Gains Tax, stamp duty, TVA and other purposes which can in certain circumstances prove advantageous. Such shares are considered as realty and are therefore subject to French succession laws.

It follows, therefore, that the purchase of property in France through the medium of such companies should be viewed with considerable circumspection. Great care must be taken in reading and fully comprehending the *Statuts* of such a company before land is bought through such a medium and enquiries should be made as to the management of the company. Certainly no shareholder who has bought land in this way should consent to the resolution to wind up and distribute in specie the property owned by the company until proper accounts have been prepared and approved by the company in General Meeting and this is an occasion when great care should be taken in the choice of proxy.

11   The Condominium

In France the condominium is governed by a basic Law of 10 July 1965, as amended by a Law of 31 December 1985 and two Statutory Instruments, Nos. 67-223 and 86-768. These apply to any building or group of buildings, parts of which are in more than one ownership. It can apply also to land owned in common by a number of owners of houses built on that land. Such ownership is known as *copropriété* and involves the ownership of a *lot* which comprises a *partie privative* and a *quote-part*. The *partie privative* will be the flat in a block or a house on a *lotissement* purchased by the owner and the *quote-part* is the proportion of the common parts of the building and its surrounding land calculated according to a number of criteria which attaches to that ownership. This right in the common parts is usually expressed in fractions of one thousand or ten thousand and is also called *tantièmes*. It is these *tantièmes* which gives a flat-owner his voting rights in the management of his block.

A *partie privative* and its *quote-part* cannot be disposed of separately. Hence the owner of a flat in France is, in terms of English law, neither a freeholder nor a leaseholder. He pays no rent but pays Service Charges. He owns the land on which his block stands, but jointly and severally with all the other flat-owners. His ownership of his flat is not limited by any term except from a practical point of view by the length of time the building will stand but in the event of its destruction, either the building will be rebuilt, in which case each flat-owner resumes occupation of his reconstructed flat, or the site will be sold, in which case he will get his share of the sale price.

A flat-owner *en copropriété* may freely sell, mortgage, give, let or otherwise deal with his flat or house. The overall management of a block of flats is in the hands of all the flat-owners themselves, who together form a *syndicat* which is a legal entity of its own. Decisions are taken in general meetings of the *syndicat*. To deal with day-to-day management, a *syndic* (Managing Agent) is appointed, and there usually is a *conseil syndical* (Executive Committee) composed of a number of flat owners. The equivalent of the lessee's covenants found in the usual long lease of a flat in Britain are the regulations contained in the *règlement de copropriété*.

In practice, a *règlement de copropriété* is made up of two parts, although each part may be prepared as separate documents. Every *lot* in a block is defined in an *état descriptif de division*. Thus each *lot* is given a number, is minutely defined by reference to its rooms and its position in the block (Building A, Staircase B, Floor C, door left or right of the lift etc.) and is given its share in the common parts, in thousandths or ten-thousandths. As a matter of practice and regret, that *lot* number is seldom, if ever, the same as the number of the flat and neither number is ever used for postal purposes. However, the Building A, Staircase B etc. description fascinates the French authorities and must be used in all communications with providers of utilities and the like.

Strictly speaking, even a building containing no more than two flats is owned *en copropriété* and requires a *syndic* and *règlement de copropriété*. Clearly, if the only two neighbours can agree on sharing the cost of maintenance, they will forgo this luxury. Not infrequently, in the case of older properties, no *règlement de copropriété* has been drawn up or pre-dates the 1965 Law. In such cases, since it is often impossible to persuade all the flat-owners to incur the expense of instructing a Notary to undertake the necessary work, it is safe to follow the requirements of the two current Laws in the day-to-day management of the building since in any event it is not permissible to derogate from most of their provisions.

The *règlement de copropriété* proper contains:
1. Regulations as to the use of all private and common parts of a building. Such regulations would typically cover the following matters:
(i) Each flat-owner may make such alterations to his flat as he wishes. This facility is restricted to the extent that if alterations would involve also a common part of the block, e.g. alterations to pipes and wires passing through the flat,

consent of the *copropriété* in general meeting is required. In very general terms, the definition of the extent of a flat is similar to that to be found in an English long lease of similar property.

(ii) No work may be carried out by a flat-owner to the exterior of the block without similar consent. This prevents individual painting of windows or doors leading to balconies or even work to balconies themselves. This can prove a nuisance when there is damage to a balcony for the owner may have to wait months for a decision. The majority of *copropriétés* require all flat-owners to have blinds of a designated pattern.

(iii) The user of any part of a block is described. Use as a private dwelling-house will not permit a commercial use but unless there is an express prohibition, a private user permits the use of the premises for professional purposes, e.g. by a doctor, lawyer etc. Thus the distinction can be fine, since use as a non-professional but not strictly commercial office is likely to be forbidden. It is common for blocks of flats to have a commercial user on the ground floor.

There is one somewhat unusual exception to these rules. A Law of 21 December 1984 permits the contravention of the user provisions in a *règlement de copropriété* in order to enable the flat-owner (or his tenant) to use the flat as the Registered Office of any company he incorporates or business he sets up which requires the use of a *siège social* for a period not exceeding two years from the date of the registration of the company or business.

(iv) The primary responsibility for the insurance of the block and its surrounding land and amenities is that of the *syndic*. The premium(s) will form part of the expenditure which goes to the make-up of the Service Charges. The flat-owner himself is required to insure in respect of his *partie privative* against such risks as are not covered by the *syndic*, e.g. public liability, damage to neighbouring property, damage to contents. Because of the frequent artificiality in the distinction between the common and private parts of a block, it is becoming more and more common for the *copropriété* to effect insurance in respect of both parts. It is therefore essential to consult the *syndic* and establish what cover he has or has not effected.

(v) Basically, each flat-owner may freely use the common parts subject to his respect of the similar right of all other flat-owners and in accordance with any internal regulations from time to time made in general meeting. These are much as one would expect to find in their English counterparts.

(vi) It is permissible to forbid flat-owners the use of certain parts of the common parts of a building, e.g. not to park cars in certain areas but it is not permissible to deprive a flat-owner of an amenity directly linked to the use of his flat, e.g. the use of a lift.

2. Definitions of the Service Charges and the proportion(s) which fall upon each flat-owner.

(i) The *quote-part* of the common parts of a building which is linked to each flat is, as has been said, of considerable significance to every flat-owner. Not only does it govern the amount of Service Charge payable in respect of his flat but it quantifies the flat-owner's voting rights at meetings of the *copropriété*. It is possible that different *quote-parts* or *tantièmes* apply on the one hand to the calculation of voting rights and on the other hand to the sharing-out of the Service Charges but this is rare. The original calculation of *quote-parts* is an extremely complex exercise which is normally done in the very early stages of the construction of a building and is based on a comparison of the value of any one part of the building with the other parts. Among other considerations, the permitted use, the situation in the block, the area and the quality of a flat all play their part but the result must never be taken as an indication of relative market values.

(ii) There may be (and frequently are) both general and special Service Charges. The law distinguishes between the expense of the maintenance and administration of a *copropriété* as a whole and that incurred in connection with an individual building in a complex or even of one part as opposed to other parts of a single building. Thus the *règlement de copropriété* may show that the owners of flats in Block A contribute in certain percentages to common expenditure but in other proportions to expenditure related solely to their block. It should be noted that such an arrangement cannot be implied from the fact that there is more than one block in a complex; it must be expressly stated in the *règlement de copropriété*, for otherwise all flat-owners will contribute towards the maintenance of all blocks.

(iii) A further difficulty in the calculation of individual Service Charges arises from the theoretical value of certain services to any particular flat. Thus, at least two factors govern the value to a flat of a lift; the floor on which it is and the number of occupants of that flat. Clearly a flat on the ground floor obtains no benefit from a lift. A collective central heating and hot water system is another fruitful source of theoretical calculations too complex to be dealt with here. Suffice it to say that most blocks built after about 1980 have individual heating and hot water systems and hence this problem is avoided.

3. Regulations for the management of the *copropriété*.

(i) These will include the appointment of the Executive Committee, the powers of the *syndic*, the convening of Meetings of flat-owners and the voting majorities required for the various types of resolutions proposed at such Meetings.

(ii) Meetings of the *copropriété* are normally called by the *syndic* both in the case of the Annual General Meeting or, if some matter of importance arises during the year, in the case of Extraordinary General Meetings. In addition, Meetings may be called when the *syndic* is required to do so by (a) the *conseil syndical* or (b) flat-owners having together not less than one quarter of the total votes of all flat-owners unless the *règlement de copropriété* indicates a lesser proportion or (c) in certain cases, the Chairman of the *conseil syndical* or some other person nominated by the Court.

(iii) All flat-owners are entitled to attend; joint owners attend by one of their number nominated to represent all. Notices of Meetings must be sent by registered AR post or by personal delivery. All *copropriétaires* normally resident out of France should either give the *syndic* their home address or appoint a proxy (see below) to receive such Notices. Failure to do this will result in Notices addressed to the vacant flat being returned by the Post Office to the *syndic*. Except in cases of emergencies, fifteen clear days notice of a Meeting must be given but by the time an undelivered Notice has found its way back to the *syndic*, the Meeting will have been held. An agenda must accompany the Notice, and in the case of many matters for discussion (e.g. consideration of Service Charge accounts, estimates for large repair items) supporting papers must accompany the Agenda. In addition to matters placed on the Agenda by the *syndic* there is a procedure for individual flat-owners also to have questions raised at a Meeting.

(iv) Every *copropriétaire* may attend a Meeting in person or by proxy. Basically, a proxy need not be another *copropriétaire*, but the *règlement de copropriété* may properly impose such limitation. Neither the *syndic* nor his spouse nor any close member of his family may act as proxy. The practice of giving the *syndic* blank proxies which he distributes at Meetings to suitable persons is common but to be deprecated. No person may act as proxy for more than three *copropriétaires* unless the total proxies he receives does not exceed, including his own votes, if any, more than five per cent of the total flat-owners' votes. Even this restriction can be overcome by including in the proxy a power to sub-delegate, since persons so appointed by a named proxy are not counted towards this maximum.

(v) In the early days of a development, when many flats may remain unsold, the developer will enjoy a large number of votes in respect of those unsold flats. In such circumstances or indeed at any time when more than one half of the total votes resides in one person, his voting rights are reduced to the number of votes in the hands of the other flat-owners, thus producing stalemate for the benefit of the otherwise outvoted.

(vi) The approval of annual accounts and works of day-to-day maintenance and management require only a simple majority vote. Certain resolutions require the majority not merely of those flat-owners present in person or by proxy but of all the flat-owners. These include the appointment and dismissal of the *syndic*, the granting to the *syndic* of certain powers normally vested in the body of the *copropriétaires*, the effecting of certain works designed to conserve energy or improve the buildings and the installation of communal TV aerials. However, in certain cases, if such a majority cannot be obtained at a Meeting, it may be adjourned to a later date when the resolution can be passed by a majority of those present at that second Meeting. Other resolutions, such as to approve improvement works, require the majority of flat-owners who together represent not less than two-thirds of the total votes which can be cast. In the case of one or two resolutions when, for example, it is sought to remove an installation such as the central heating system, the unanimous vote of all the flat-owners is required.

(vii) In the case of the total or partial destruction of a building by fire or from some other cause, the circumstances in which rebuilding takes place are to be found in the *règlement de copropriété*, which do not need to follow the rules laid down by the Law of 10 July 1965 but more often than not in fact do so. In such case, a General Meeting of all the flat-owners whose building has been destroyed or damaged may by a simple majority decide to rebuild or repair the damage. If less than half a building is destroyed or damaged, a simple majority of the flat-owners who have suffered can require rebuilding or repair of the destroyed or damaged part of the building. The cost of the work of rebuilding or repair is found from the flat-owners in the building in the same proportion as they contributed to Service Charges but it is to be expected that insurance moneys will cover this expenditure.

No one should complete the purchase of a flat without having seen and studied and having some appreciation of the *règlement de copropriété* which relates to it. Alas, this is a counsel of perfection and many purchases are in fact completed without the buyer seeing the document or being advised as to its contents. The law stipulates that a purchaser is deemed to have notice of the contents of every *règlement de copropriété* filed at the Land Registry. Since most are so registered, many purchasers become bound on completion by rules and regulations of which, if they are not French, they know nothing and this despite the requirement of the 1965 Statutory Instrument that every *acte de vente* contain a statement that the purchaser has knowledge of the contents of every registered *règlement de copropriété* and of the *état descriptif* and of any modifications of either document. Even if these documents have not been registered, a buyer who states in the *acte de vente* that he knows their contents and agrees to be bound by them is so bound.

Service Charges are usually paid by instalments in advance calculated by reference to the budget for the ensuing year. Subject to any provision in the *règlement de copropriété* or to any decision of a General Meeting, an instalment may not exceed one half of the budget figure. The budget is agreed to at the Meeting which approves the accounts for the year past. Adjustments are made annually with the resultant debits or credits being applied to the following year. Such instalments are intended for the day-to-day running of the *copropriété* or for expenses specifically voted at a meeting. However, it is not uncommon for a *copropriété* to have a reserve fund to meet unexpected expenses to which single, regular or irregular contributions are made by flat-owners. Reference must normally be made to the *règlement de copropriété* in order to discover the circumstances in which such payments can be required from flat-owners.

Failure to pay Service Charges can have several results. In the first place, the Law states that, unless the *règlement de copropriété* provides otherwise, interest at the 'legal rate' becomes payable. The 'legal rate' is fixed annually by the Banque de France and is linked to the French equivalent of Base Rate. In addition, the *règlement de copropriété* may provide for additional penal interest. If the *syndic* is finally obliged to have recourse to legal action to recover Service Charges, he may without the prior authority of a General Meeting institute any of the straightforward procedures equivalent to the issue of a writ or he may obtain a *saisie-arrêt* over cash assets of the defaulting flat-owner. Other remedies are available. The *copropriété* may distrain on the contents of a flat, and if the flat is let unfurnished, the rent obtained can also be made subject to distraint. He may register a charge against the flat for unpaid Service Charges (such a course of action is not by any means unknown), which can ultimately lead to a sale by the Court.

All sales must be notified to the *syndic*. This is normally done by the Notary acting for the vendor or the sole Notary acting. Until this notification is given, the sale is ineffective *vis à vis* the *copropriété*, and the seller remains liable to the *syndic*. Such notice normally results in the *syndic* advising the

Notary of the amount due by way of Service Charge to the date of completion and claiming payment out of the proceeds of sale. This is usually the final method of recovering unpaid Service Charges.

It is not without interest to consider how effective is the system of *copropriété* in France. France is not, of course, the only country where the condominium system is used and it would seem that, in the long run, it is the national character which decides whether the idea suits a country or not. The excesses of the US system which allows 'undesirable' purchasers to be kept from buying is not known in France, since property *en copropriété* is freely transferable without reference to the *syndicat*. The condominium exists in Italy where the most ingenious and charming methods are used to overcome the more irritating provisions of the law. However, it is a system which requires, if it is to function well, that on the whole those who make use of it are not only not quarrelsome by nature but well versed in the art of 'give and take'.

For the English buyer, to whom the system is novel, it has certain disadvantages. Compared with the purchase of flats by way of the long lease, there is no lessor-lessee relationship, so there is no single person against whom all the lessees can join to attack. It is true that in the case of some English blocks the management is vested in a company whose shareholders are the lessees themselves but this seems to be limited to smaller blocks. The French system imposes, in every case, management by an entity composed of the flat-owners themselves. Thus, whilst in England the Tenants Associations and other statutory means of protection for flat-owners are for the benefit of the body of flat-owners in a block commonly against a third-party enemy, under the French system the law protects flat-owners in a block inevitably against each other. By nature the French are disputatious and upholders of their own rights whilst evincing less interest in the rights of others. Hence it is inevitable that meeting of flat-owners tend to reflect these characteristics rather than adequately deal with management problems. Moreover, for reasons which still remain unexplained, the profession of *syndic* produces in very many cases a standard of management which would be totally unacceptable in England.

In addition, most English flat-owners are to be found in

those parts of France which are essentially holiday areas. Thus few flat-owners are permanent residents and it is surprising how the standard of management rises when there is a reasonable number of round-the-year residents. Meetings of flat-owners are, of course, carried on in French and are not easy to follow. In many cases there are more absentee than attending flat-owners and many decisions go by default. Service Charge accounts are often very difficult to follow and complaints to a *syndic* are not infrequently ignored.

It is therefore necessary to add a word of advice to the English flat-owner in France. Unless he is a permanent resident and fluent in French, he should appoint a permanent proxy in France to exercise his rights as *copropriétaire* and act for him in all problems where the *syndic* is concerned.

12 Non-Commercial Leases

Leases of private dwelling-houses in France are subject to either (i) a Rent Restriction Law of 1948 or (ii) to *la Loi Méhaignerie* of 23 December 1986 as amended by the Law of 6 July 1989, which are together referred to in this Chapter as 'the current Law' or they are free of any statutory restriction.

It is not considered necessary to deal with the 1948 Law, the application of which is unlikely to extend to property rented by or to the non-French.

The current Law does not apply to the following lettings, which are however subject to the standard provisions of the Code Civil relating to leases:

(i) furnished lettings of whatever kind and irrespective of whether the landlord or tenant is a private individual or corporation;

(ii) holiday lettings. The Law uses the expression '*location à caractère saissonière*', and it is generally accepted that this implies two distinct requirements. A letting must be for a short period – one or two weeks or, if longer, for at least a period which does not overrun 'the season'. Secondly, the reference to '*saison*' implies that this exemption refers primarily to places where there is a 'season' e.g. ski resorts, spas, seaside areas. Hence, to be safely outside the Law, a letting should be of premises in a place which has a 'season', and the term should not extend beyond its end;

(iii) lettings of '*résidences secondaires*'. The quality of *résidence secondaire* depends on the situation of the tenant and not of the landlord. Such a letting is to a tenant who has a principal residence elsewhere and not by a landlord of his second home;

(iv) service tenancies;

(v) garages and parking spaces which do not form part of a private dwelling-house or block of flats not let together with the dwelling-house or a flat in the block.

Leases falling within the above categories are subject to the following basic provisions, which the parties are at liberty to vary as they wish:

1. The letting need not be in writing; the term may be for any fixed period or indeterminate, and the rent is not controlled in any way, nor is any norm applicable.

2. The landlord may impose financial burdens on a tenant which he may not do in the case of a 1986 law lease. For example, he may require his tenant to pay *taxe foncière*, which, being a tax on the ownership of land, is normally payable by a landlord.

3. The tenant is liable for damage caused to the premises by him and members of his family, his invitees and agents and can only avoid this liability if he can prove that there was no default on his or their part, that he had taken every precaution necessary to prevent the damage or that it occurred by *force majeur*. A tenant is liable for damage by fire except in certain cases provided for by the Code Civil. Normally the tenancy agreement will require the tenant to insure but the law itself does not.

4. In connection with the respective liabilities of landlord and tenant, the framers of the Code Civil had to bear in mind the letting of flats rather than of houses. In fact a considerably higher proportion of the population in France lives in flats than in England and has done for centuries. The landlord is required to let his premises in a state of good repair subject to any provision to the contrary in the tenancy agreement. He undertakes to give quiet enjoyment (including a liability for the acts of third parties). With stark simplicity, Article 1720 of the Code Civil requires a landlord to undertake 'all repairs which may become necessary during the term other than those which are the obligation of a tenant'.

Basically, a tenant is liable for all interior repairs other than those which are rendered necessary by the age of the building or *force majeure* or by reason of the landlord's failure to maintain the structure of the building. Article 1724 of the Code Civil requires a tenant to permit entry to a landlord to carry out repairs to the demised premises which are urgent and cannot be put off to the end of the term 'whatever may be the nuisance caused thereby and notwithstanding that [the tenant] may be deprived of the use of part of the premises'. Such repairs are those for which a landlord is liable or in respect of which a tenant is in default but from a practical point of view it must be remembered that the landlord of a flat will himself be a *copropriétaire*, so that his tenant is very much in the position of a sub-tenant under an English sub-lease who covenants to allow a head landlord entry to the premises to carry out repairs. The Code Civil provides that a tenant can require a reduction of rent if the works continue for more than forty days and can surrender his tenancy if the works render the premises inhabitable. However, these provisions can be varied by agreement and usually are, to the further detriment of the tenant.

5. It is customary not to permit assignments but underlettings are frequently permitted. On a permitted assignment, notice should be given to the landlord. The original tenant and each successive assignee remain liable to the landlord for due performance of the terms of the letting.

A large proportion of lettings in France are to some extent subject to the current Law. Some are controlled as to rent and some are not but otherwise most are within the scope of the current Law. The Law as it stands represents what is left of a Socialist Law passed in the early 1980s intended to be for the protection of tenants which resulted, as had been predicted, in the virtual disappearance of the letting market. Subsequently, that Law was much amended in favour of landlords as to rent control and security of tenure by the following right-wing government whilst the present Law shows a gentle swing back in favour of the tenant. However, the original Law served also as a Landlord and Tenant Act proper regulating the rights and liabilities of the parties to a lease. Such provisions, which were much needed, have remained in the main unaltered.

For the current Law to apply, the premises in question must be let (i) unfurnished (ii) as a private dwelling-house or for a mixed professional and private user (lettings for mixed private and commercial user are dealt with under rules applying to commercial lettings) and (iii) as the principal residence of the lessee. The provisions of the current Law being *d'ordre public*, the parties cannot contract out of them. Provisions in a lease which are contrary to the Law are, in the view of some, *ab initio* void or, in the view of others, voidable at the instance of the tenant only. In some cases, as in the omission of certain facts required to be recited in a lease, the lease is neither void nor voidable but either party can require the insertion of what has been omitted.

The following are the main provisions of the current Law:

1. Every lease where the landlord is a company must be for a term of at least six years and where the landlord is a private individual for a term of at least three years. However, when the lessor is a private individual and the lease states precise reasons of a personal nature which would make it essential for him to retake possession before the expiry of three years, the term may be for less than three years but for not less than one year. There are special provisions also where the lessee is a family company or the premises are held *en indivision*.

2. All costs of the grant of the lease must be borne equally between landlord and tenant.

3. The rent of some flats is controlled and of some is free. Among those whose rents are not controlled are new flats and flats which are vacant and have been brought up to the standard defined by the Statutory Instrument of 26 August 1987 (see 10 below). Flats the rents of which are subject to control are those not designated as free of control if the rent asked exceeds the rent paid by the immediately previous tenant and when the lease is not an original lease but one granted on a renewal of the letting. Rents in these cases may be fixed by a special Tribunal.

4. Every lease must be in writing but it need not be by *acte authentique*. It may be s.s.p. In theory, a verbal letting is void but either party can request the other to reduce the letting to writing and on a refusal, application can be made to the court for an order in appropriate terms.

5. Every lease must contain (a) the date of the commencement of the term (b) a complete description of the demised premises and its fixtures and fittings (c) the permitted user of the premises (d) a description of any appurtenances or items of which the lessee will have (i) exclusive use and (ii) use in common with others during the term (e) the rent reserved and times for payment and provisions (if any) for revision and (f) provisions for a deposit (if any).

6. A deposit may be asked for by the landlord unless the rent is payable at least three monthly in advance. A deposit may not exceed two months' rent. This deposit must be refunded within two months of the determination of the lease from whatever cause. This is a rule liable to considerable non-observance and it is often sensible to cease to pay rent in an amount equal to the deposit during the last month or so of the letting.

7. Any clause in a lease requiring the payment of rent by direct debit of the tenant's bank account or by deduction from the tenant's salary or to be secured by promissory notes or bills of exchange is void, as is any clause requiring the tenant to insure the premises with a company of the landlord's choice. Certain clauses relating to methods of charging for repairs or which oblige the tenant to receive prospective tenants or purchasers for periods of more than two hours per working day or which provide for forfeiture for breaches of convenant other than for the non-payment of rent are void. So is a clause restricting the tenant's political, trade union or religious activities although, since a tenant may only use the premises for its permitted user, which certainly would not include the holding of trade union meetings or religious gatherings, the provision seems of little practical value other than to pay lip service to '*liberté*'.

8. The landlord must ensure that the demised premises are in a good state of repair at the commencement of the term. It is not obligatory to have a Schedule of Condition on taking possession but a wise tenant will insist on one, for otherwise he will be presumed to have taken the premises in a good state of repair whatever their true state may be. Likewise, a Schedule of Dilapidations is desirable at the end of the term. These may be prepared by a *huissier* or by the parties themselves.

9. The tenant is required to insure against all risks for which he is liable as tenant.

10. The primary liability of the tenant is 'peaceably to occupy the premises in accordance with the permitted user', the landlord undertaking to give quiet enjoyment. The landlord's repairing liability is to maintain the premises in a state which will enable it to be used for the purposes for which it was let and to undertake all such repairs other than

those for which the tenant is liable in order to maintain the premises in a normal state of repair. A Statutory Instrument of 26 August 1987 lists all the repairs for which a tenant is liable save to the extent that such repairs are rendered necessary by reason of the age of or faults of construction of the building or *force majeure*.

It is not safe to translate the technical terms relating to repairs in a French lease by the use of the phrases so commonly found in repairing covenants in English leases. It may well be that the French take a somewhat more pragmatic view of repairing liabilities than clearly have the Judges in England over a period of years. However, from a wholly practical point of view, it can be said that in the long run most items of repair are likely to fall initially on the tenant coupled with the hope that the cost of some at least can be recouped. Landlords in France, frequently through their managing agents, tend to avoid their liabilities, at least for long enough for it to become necessary for tenants to have the work done initially at their own cost and in this connection tenants should resort to a *constat d'huissier* of the pre-repair situation if they want to avoid a denial by their landlord that any work was necessary or (receipted bills notwithstanding) carried out.

There is another problem. Very many lettings are of flats where the landlord is himself no more than a *copropriétaire*. It may well be that to comply with his repairing liability as a landlord either he needs the consent of the *copropriété* or the repair is one which can only be carried out by the *copropriété* itself. Such a situation does not lend itself to early decisions.

11. The Statutory Instrument of 26 August 1987 referred to above also lists the items which go to the make-up of the landlord's Service Charges and which may be recovered from the tenant. In general terms, these items refer to the day-to-day running and maintenance of lifts, hot and cold water and central heating systems, maintenance of the interior common parts of the building of which the demised premise form part, maintenance of the exterior amenities of the building (swimming-pools, gardens, lighting, security etc.) and various other items. Reimbursement of the proper amount from a tenant can only be obtained against receipts or other proof of payment. The usual practice is for the lease

to provide for a regular payment on account of these *charges* and for an annual adjustment to be made against production of or extracts from the *syndic*'s Service Charge accounts rendered to the landlord.

12. No lease may be assigned nor may sub-lettings be created without the consent in writing of the landlord. In this connection, it should be noted that a permitted sub-letting is outside the scope of the current Law but the rent charged to a subtenant may not exceed that charged to the head tenant.

13. In derogation of the normal provision that a lease forms part of the tenant's estate on his death, under the current Law certain persons have a prior claim on that lease and can require it to be transferred to them. These persons include the surviving spouse, ascendants or descendants of the tenant, certain persons in the care of the deceased tenant and any person (and his or her issue) openly and to the knowledge of all living with but not married to the deceased tenant.

14. At any time during the term of a lease, the tenant may give three months notice to quit in accordance with the provisions of the lease. This will normally be by registered AR letter or by *huissier*. However, the period is reduced to one month if the tenant loses or changes his employment or if he is over sixty and his state of health requires a change of residence. A landlord may give notice to quit on the grounds of the tenant's breach of his obligations but if the breach is the non-payment of rent or other money payment, the tenant may apply to the Court within two months for suspension of the notice on such terms as the Judge may think fit.

15. Normally, a tenant should give formal notice to quit three months before the expiry of his lease if he is not seeking a renewal. A landlord intending not to renew a lease must give six months notice of that intention which can be for one of the following reasons:

(i) That the landlord intends to sell the premises provided that the purchaser is not a relation as close as the third degree and that the purchaser occupies the premises when bought for at least two years. In such a case, a tenant has a right of pre-emption to be exercised within two months of receipt of the notice after which the right becomes void.

(ii) That the landlord requires the premises for his own occupation or for that of his spouse or of his *concubin notoire* of at least one year's standing at the date of the service of the notice to quit or for his parents or issue or those of his spouse or *concubin notoire*.

No notice on these grounds may be served on a tenant who is aged more than seventy and whose income is less than one and half times SMIC (see Glossary) unless either (a) 'suitable' alternative accommodation is offered to him or (b) the landlord is a private individual aged more than sixty or (c) if the income of the landlord is less than one-and-a-half times SMIC.

(iii) That the landlord has 'proper and serious' grounds. Such grounds according to the Law of 6 July 1989 would be the breach of any of the tenant's obligations as to which the Court must pronounce.

16. If, at the expiration of a lease, the landlord (i) fails to serve a notice to quit on the grounds mentioned above or (ii) does not in the case of a lease at a manifestly low lease make an offer of renewal at a proper rent, the lease is automatically renewed for a period of three years if the landlord is a private individual or six years if it is a company. A landlord who wishes to renew a lease but at a proper rent must give six months notice of that intention reciting in the notice the clauses of the Law which refer to such an event. The new rent will be that fixed by reference to rents for comparable premises in the neighbourhood. The tenant may either accept the offer or have recourse to the Tribunal or take no action within the prescribed time limits when the lease will determine.

The grant of a lease at a rent exceeding what is virtually a peppercorn involves the annual payment of *droit de bail* which is charged *ad valorem* on the rent. This small tax is borne by the tenant. An additional *droit de bail* in the case of building built before 1975 is always borne by the landlord.

The number of non-commercial leases prepared or even 'vetted' by lawyers in France must be minimal. The almost inevitable procedure is for the landlord's Agent to hand over a printed form of lease and expect the tenant to sign it there and then. This is not to say that amendments will not be allowed, so long (usually) as they do not throw extra burdens on the landlord but that leaves very little scope for negotiation. Non-French tenants are strongly advised not to execute leases before getting proper advice, not so much because this will result in alterations being made but because at least they will then know what their liabilities in fact will be.

For the foreigner, references can prove to be a puzzle as well as a nuisance. Letting Agents will ask for a variety of information which may include such items as the last six months' rent receipts of one's previous flat, one or more year's tax returns or receipts, and salary slips. Bank references are not usually asked for, since French banks normally will not give written references. Prospective non-French tenants should not be dismayed, particularly if they have only recently arrived in France but equally should not without demur offer information of this kind. Usually considerably less than what was asked for and often in a different form will be accepted if language difficulties do not inhibit discussion.

Parties to leases are frequently required by law to address each other by registered AR letter. Even when the law does not so require, they should use this means of communication in all dealings with their landlord or his agent. Indeed, every legal or business communication of any significance in France, irrespective of who is the sender and who the recipient, should go by registered AR post, whether the law requires it or not. French offices have the habit of not receiving letters, which allows them not to reply to them and the only manner in which the sender of a letter can protect himself, often with considerable need to do so, is by the use of this very expensive form of post.

13   *Sales* En Viager

Among the more interesting transactions fairly widely used in France and virtually unknown in England is the transaction *en viager*. The expression *viager* has its origin in the now obsolete French word *viage* meaning 'lifetime'. Transactions of this kind are defined in the Code Civil as those which may involve either realty or personalty, 'the burdens and benefits of which in so far as they affect one or more of the parties, depend upon the happening of an uncertain event'. Such an event, if indeed it was ever any other, is now taken to be the death of one or more persons, be they parties to the transaction or other lives. Depending as they do upon an element of risk, Articles 1964 to 1983 of the Code Civil, which lay down the rules applicable to transactions *en viager*, are to be found in that part of the Code devoted to contracts of insurance and betting and gaming contracts.

Today, transactions *en viager* are almost exclusively limited to sales of land. Notwithstanding that essentially such a sale is one under which the price is paid by instalments during the existence of a named life and that such an annuity is charged against the land sold, nothing in the Code Civil requires that the whole of the sale price should be by way of annuity or that vacant possession of the property sold should be given on completion. In fact, the modern *viager* transaction usually provides for a part of the sale price to be paid on completion (*le bouquet*) and the balance to be paid by monthly instalments (*la rente viagère*). More often than not, the seller remains in occupation until his death and is the life in being to which the annuity is linked. There are also sales *en viager* which give immediate possession and some are pure investments on the part of a buyer rather than initiated as a means of assistance to the seller.

Frequently, of course, a sale *en viager* will be of property occupied by an elderly couple where theirs will be the lives in being and the *rente* will be payable on a joint life and survivor basis. The annuity can even be linked to the 'life' of a company (French companies are usually formed for a definite period of time) provided that this does not exceed thirty years.

The basic sale price is the market price with vacant possession discounted if the buyer does not take vacant possession. Further adjustment must also be made to take account of how the price is split between *bouquet* and *rente* and these calculations are usually dealt with by specialists in sales *en viager*. It is also possible to index a *rente* and whether the sale document provides for this or not also affects the final price. It must be remembered, however, that the essence of a sale *en viager* is that it must involve an element of risk. Hence the Courts in France have held that a sale by a person whose expectation of life is unreasonably short by reason of ill-health is void, for there is no genuine risk element involved. Likewise the sale of any capital asset *en viager* at a price which produces for the seller less or even the same as the asset, had it not been sold, could have produced by way of income at normal market rates is void on the ground that the seller did not need to sell in order to obtain what he would have received from the proceeds of the sale.

A sale with vacant possession is a *viager libre*; a sale subject to the continued occupation of the seller or (much less usually) a third party is a *viager occupé*. Here again, there is an element involved which may affect the sale price, for occupation on a sale *en viager occupé* may be by virtue of a life interest or by a mere right of occupation and whilst both are considered to be interests in land, the difference between them is significant.

A life tenant has powers of leasing; a mere occupier has not. The length of the term which a life tenant may grant is limited by law, but if such a term has not expired at the death of the life to whom the annuity period is linked, the purchaser cannot take possession until expiry of that term. A life tenant may assign or charge his interest but a mere occupier may not and there are certain advantages for the life tenant in the case of agricultural property in that he may enjoy all the rents and profits of such property whilst a mere occupant may retain only what is requisite for himself and his family.

As to the rights and obligations of the seller/life tenant or occupier on the one hand and the buyer/reversioner on the other, they do not in practice differ much from the effect of the covenants to be found in an English lease where the lessee has a full internal repairing liability. The life tenant/ occupier's liability is, to quote the delightful but untranslatable French phrase, to use the property *en bon père de famille*. He must abide by the permitted user, which in the case of agricultural land includes the obligation to keep it in good heart and condition. He is responsible for all internal repairs and certain limited external repairs such as drains and soil pipes. He is, of course, responsible for all usual annual charges and outgoings.

The buyer/reversioner is liable generally for external and main structural repairs but there have been curious judgments which cloud over the simplicity of this distinction. Thus repairs to the internal floors of a house have been held to be structural and the liability of the purchaser/reversioner but repairs to external stonework to be the liability of the life tenant/occupier. Moreover, a life tenant/occupier cannot compel compliance by a buyer/reversioner with his repairing liabilities but a life tenant/occupier who carries out repairs which are the obligation of the buyer/reversioner can recover the cost of so doing at the end of the life tenancy or period of occupation to the extent that such repairs have increased the value of the property. French law provides no obligation on the part of either party to rebuild any part of the property which decays by reason of its age or is destroyed by act of God. No compensation is available for improvements as opposed to repairs. Any of these provisions may be varied by agreement between the parties but such variations take effect *inter partes* only and do not affect third parties.

An occupant retaining possession of property sold *en viager* as opposed to a life tenant must prior to taking occupation i.e. on completion of the sale, provide a suitable guarantee for the performance of his obligations during the period of his occupancy. When his right to remain in occupation comes to an end, the buyer/reversioner may obtain a possession order if this is necessary. A life interest normally determines on merger with the reversion i.e. on the death of the only life or the survivor of more than one life. It determines also if it is not exercised for a period of thirty years from the date of its creation or in event of the total destruction of the property. It may also be determined by the Court at the instance of the buyer/reversioner for gross breaches of the life tenant's obligations.

Annuity payments may as has been indicated, be indexed, and a variety of indices are available. Gold clauses are forbidden nor may an annuity be linked to foreign exchange rates or to any devaluation of the French franc. Sometimes a minimum variation in an index is required to trigger off a variation in the annuity and indexation works downwards as well as upwards. Annuities accrue on a daily basis but, unless so made in the sale document, are not apportionable on death. As is normal, annuity payments are made against certificates that the life in question is alive and these can be obtained from the local *mairie* or Bank Manager or a Notary.

By law, there is only one remedy for non-payment of the annuity. The seller/life tenant may levy execution on the goods of the purchaser/reversioner in an amount sufficient to allow him to buy an annuity similar to that to which he is entitled under the sale arrangements. This is considered hardly practical and sale documents usually contain the provision that default in payment of the annuity entitles the seller to put an end to the *viager* arrangements and revest the property in himself.

A sale *en viager* unless it qualifies for exemption on the same grounds as any other sale is subject to Capital Gains Tax calculated by reference to the capitalized value of the *rente viagère* plus the *bouquet*. The annuity is treated an unearned income in the hands of the recipient but, as in the UK, there is a non-taxable capital element involved dependent on the age of the life in question. However, unlike the UK, this capital element is tax-free in the case of all annuities and not only those granted 'in the ordinary course of the business of granting annuities'.

The situation on death is as might be expected. The seller/tenant for life owns no property on which death duties can be levied except to the extent that he has not spent all his *bouquet*. However, as in the UK, there are certain tax avoidance provisions designed to catch inter-family transactions and some of these can apply to *en viager* transactions. As for the purchaser/reversioner, death duties will be payable in France on the value of his reversion in a *viager occupé* property save that, exceptionally, there is total exemption in respect of a surviving spouse.

It is important not to overlook *viager* transactions as either unsuitable for or unavailable to English purchasers or as a method in certain circumstances of disposing of real property in France by English owners. For persons who intend to retire to France at some future date but who want to secure a suitable property at today's prices, a purchase *en viager* may prove suitable. It has the additional attraction that only a proportion of the price need be found on completion, the balance being paid over a period of time. Every purchaser on this basis would, of course, be well advised to consider insuring against the possibility of the life in question living beyond its normal expectancy.

From an existing owner's point of view, a sale *en viager* can achieve a number of objectives. It can, in the first place, release capital to him, which, in the case of those living on a fixed income, can be helpful. It can also in appropriate circumstances reduce his French death duty liabilities. Finally, on the assumption that the owner is not domiciled in France, a sale *en viager* is a method of turning realty into personalty and avoiding the application of French rules of succession.

The following extract from an French article on *viager* transactions explains with admirable clarity the uses to which this type of transaction may be put and, incidentally, albeit unintentionally, provides a valuable glimpse of the French involved in property transactions.

Hence older vendors, in order to improve their standard of living, have no alternative but to contemplate a sale *en viager* ... To be without children is not, however, an absolute condition for such a transaction but from a sentimental and perhaps from a moral point of view, one must suppose that in the majority of cases people with children and grandchildren will not dispose of their assets irretrievably without drastic need and without first offering that capital to their children in exchange for financial assistance of an income nature ... To sell capital *en viager* is to some extent to profit to the detriment of one's heirs. However, since as a matter of principle one does not perpetuate a difficult financial situation merely to 'feather-bed' one's heirs, the transaction is a perfectly legitimate and moral one in many cases, subject only to the comments made above, 'for the law ought not systematically to trample on natural and traditional family sentiments'.

14   Time-Sharing

Strictly speaking, this method of ownership finds no place in a book on real property law, for under French law it is personalty. However, it has become sufficiently popular and sufficiently open to abuses to merit inclusion.

Time-sharing first made its appearance in France in 1966. Twenty years later, there were in France some 80,000 owners of time-shares in property which was French-owned in about one-tenth that number of flats. It cannot therefore be said that the French have taken to this concept with great enthusiasm, but there are sellers and buyers of time-shares in property in France who are not of French nationality and include among their number the British. Its attraction lies not only in that the use of a flat for limited periods in every year may be bought at low cost but in the fact that time-ownership frequently enables the time-sharer from time to time to exchange his flat for another in another country and so enlarge considerably the area in which he may take his holidays.

Time-sharing is known by a variety of names in France. *Multipropriété*, which is the name under which it was first commercialized, has blossomed into *poly-, inter-, pluri-* or *spacio-temporelle-propriété*, whilst developers who are perhaps slightly more scrupulous in their use of the word 'property' have resorted to *multijouissance* in order to avoid the implications which use of the former connotes. Until 1986 time-sharers could look to very little protection from the law. Even now, the Law of 6 January 1986, which represents a brave attempt to give that protection, will not necessarily achieve its ends, for its use is not obligatory as a vehicle for time-sharing. It must be assumed that public demand will eventually ensure its universal use and no intending time-sharer should readily, if at all, buy a time-share under the old pattern of things.

The Law creates a new type of company whose object is the purchase, construction or alteration of a building intended solely for time-sharing purposes. The company may be in the form of a *société anonyme* or a *société à responsabilité limitée*, both of which are the French equivalents of the English limited liability company, or of a *société civile*, which provides no such protection for the shareholder. The administration of a *société civile* is so simple compared with that of an SA or an SARL that it is inevitable that it will always be chosen for this purpose. The legislature has therefore deemed it necessary to make a special exception to the rule relating to the liability of shareholders of a *société civile* to its creditors (see page 77) and to enact that such liability will be limited, as in England to the capital invested, i.e. the price of the shares or, since ownership of the shares gives the time-sharing rights, to the purchase price of such rights.

In general terms, the Law has taken the rules which apply to *sociétés d'attribution* (see Chapter 10) and welded to them the rules which apply to the management of property *en copropriété*. The following is the result.

1. The company marketing the sale of time-shares will issue shares, which may only be in registered form. Indeed, they are to be marked 'not negotiable', presumably to indicate that they are not bearers for they are freely transferable within the provisions of the company's Articles.

2. The issue of the shares will be by way of an *acte* which must contain certain information and it is strongly to be recommended that the *acte* be a notarial document. The contents of this document are referred to below.

3. Each share or, more probably, block of shares will carry with it the right to the occupation of a particular part of the building owned by the company for a limited period between given dates in every year.

4. Shares may be transferred by *acte s.s.p.* or preferably by *acte authentique*.

5. Transfers must be notified to the company at the cost of the transferee. Shares in respect of which any moneys are owing to the company cannot be transferred unless, in the

case of a transfer for value, the transferee's undertaking to be responsible directly to the company in the place of the transferor is accepted. Transfers by way of gift require the prior consent of the company.

6. If shares are transferred to transferees who are not existing shareholders prior to completion of the building owned by the company and the installation in it of all necessary equipment, the transferor must provide a guarantee from a suitable bank or insurance company against the failure of one or more of the shareholders to pay calls from time to time due in respect of their shareholdings, i.e. towards the cost of building, renovation etc.

The purchase document, whether it covers the initial allotment of shares or is a transfer of shares from an existing to a new shareholder must include:

(i) a clear description of the building and of the part to which the shares acquired give the right of occupation;

(ii) a description of the period(s) of permitted occupation;

(iii) the sale price, including details of any payments remaining to be made to the company in respect of the purchase price or the cost of construction of the building;

(iv) in the case of a transfer by an existing shareholder, details of the liabilities of the transferor *vis à vis* the company (if any) certified as correct by the company.

The company on allotment and the transferor on subsequent transfers must provide the allottee or transferee, as the case may be, with:

(i) copies of the Memorandum and Articles of the company, of the document dividing the building into its various time-sharing parts, of the document setting out the entitlement of the shares to occupancy of those parts and of the rules and regulations dealing with the occupation and management of the building;

(ii) technical information relating to services installed in the building;

(iii) a copy of the company's last audited accounts;

(iv) details of the Service Charges paid in the previous financial year of the company by the owner of the shares to be sold or, if the allotment or transfer takes place during the first year of the company's existence, an estimate of this liability;

(v) the inventory of the contents of the flat to the occupation of which the shares in question give right.

Such documents should be annexed to the *acte* and a copy given to the allottee or transferee as the case may be.

Special rules apply to an allotment or transfer of shares where the building is either in the course of construction or is being renovated when the cost of such works exceeds fifty per cent of the purchase price of the property by the company. In such circumstances, an allottee or transferee is entitled to evidence that (i) the company has entered into either a building development contract in terms required by statute or a contract for the purchase of the building *en l'état futur d'achèvement* (see Chapter 4) and has effected proper cover to guarantee completion of the building works and (ii) that it has effected cover to provide any balance of the cost of purchase, building, renovation etc. the payment of which is made necessary by reason of the default of any shareholder. In the case of a transfer of shares at a time when these provisions apply, it is assumed that a transferee is entitled to obtain from his transferor and not from the company evidence of the existence of these protective arrangements.

Regulations made by the company will govern the day-to-day use of flats – the date and hour when occupation may be taken, liability for damage to a flat, its user etc. Exchanges of flats will normally be permitted between shareholders, but the responsibility towards the company remains that of the shareholder who has the right to occupy the flat by virtue of his shareholding. It is not lawful to forbid letting or parting with possession of a flat to a non-shareholder during the permitted period of occupancy but the shareholder will, of course, remain liable to the company for its use during that period. How difficult it is to borrow to buy a time-share is another matter. The underlying asset – the right to occupy a flat – is not realty and cannot be mortgaged. The shares can be charged to a lender as security but it seems unlikely that a Bank or other institution willing to make a loan for such a purpose against such security could easily be found.

Service Charges are payable by each shareholder. Basically,

these will be calculated as they would for a block owned *en copropriété* and divided out among shareholders equitably but will, of course, include an amount for the use of the furnishings and other contents of each flat. Normally a shareholder will be expected to make a payment on account and pay, as in a condominium, towards all the cost of management, maintenance and the provision of amenities. A shareholder in arrears with his Service Charge payments may be refused access to his flat, and as a final sanction his shares can be forfeited and sold if a two-thirds majority of the shareholders in General Meeting so resolves.

Management of the company will, in the case of a *société civile*, be provided by the *gérant(s)*, who may be removed by a simple majority vote of the shareholders.

A General Meeting of the shareholders must be held at least once a year. Shareholders owning at least twenty per cent of the issued share may convene a Meeting, which must be held within three months of being convened. Fifteen days notice at least of Meetings must be given, during which period shareholders are entitled to copies of the company's accounts and to consult the register of shareholders.

A shareholder may vote in person or by proxy and the Articles may provide for voting by correspondence. A proxy may be a person or corporation and need not be a shareholder of the company. All the shareholders who have the right to occupy flats at the same time in any year may appoint a proxy for periods of three years at a time to represent them as a group but such an appointment does not affect the right of each individual shareholder to be present in person or to appoint his own proxy to attend Meetings. A shareholder's general voting rights will depend on the number of shares he owns except that, if his liability to pay Service Charges is based on a different proportion, it is that proportion which applies to all questions relating to Service Charges. As is to be expected, simple majorities carry many resolutions but some, such as the amendment of the Articles, require a larger majority.

On expiration of the period for which the company was incorporated or at some prior date if so resolved by the shareholders, the company will be wound up and the net assets divided among the shareholders. The Articles will normally forbid a distribution in specie on liquidation.

As has been said, the asset acquired by a time-sharer, namely shares in a French company, is personalty. Assuming therefore that the shareholder is not domiciled in France, which for an English shareholder is the most likely situation, these shares will pass on his death under English and not French law.

Little can be said as to the original system designed for time-sharing in France. It depended on no more than a contractual right to occupy a flat for a given period of time between two dates (*jouissance*) and provided little means of enforcing the provision of all those amenities without which occupation by a time-sharer of his flat would be less than satisfactory. How effectively the time-sharer could enforce such rights as he had and, in certain cases when the sellers of time-shares are not French based, where he could enforce them, was and must remain a matter for speculation. What is too seldom appreciated is that the non-French seller of time-shares may well be not the owner of the block in which time-shares are for sale but the owner of only one or two flats in the block. This, in the light of the rules relating to the management of the condominium in France, effectively means that the seller of time-shares who will probably manage the property in which he has sold these rights will himself be at the mercy of the *copropriété*, and this removes the time-sharer too far from the source of real management for comfort in law or in practice.

There has also appeared in France a novel form of time-sharing called *bi-propriété*. This usually involves the full legal ownership of the flat or house in question *en indivision* (see Chapter 9) with one other person and gives a six-month right of occupation per year to each co-owner. Sometimes this result is achieved through the medium of a *société civile* but not in the form of a company created under the 1986 Law referred to earlier in this chapter and this method may or may not give rise to the ownership of land as opposed to personalty. It is hard to believe that this type of time-sharing will become very popular but it does serve a special need. For obvious reasons, no English buyer on such a basis should proceed without the fullest advice.

15   *Auction Sales*

It is perhaps not likely that many purchases in France will be made at auction but since on occasion there are bargains to be had and since the system has certain important differences from that in force in England, the French rules merit consideration.

Sales by auction in France fall into two categories depending upon whether this method of sale has been chosen by a seller on advice or whether the law requires its use. Sales which must by law be by auction are *ventes judiciares* and include sales by a mortgagee under the equivalent of a foreclosure order, sales of property belonging to a person who is not *sui juris*, sales of property in joint ownership where there is disaccord among the joint owners and in certain circumstances, sales during the course of the administration of the estates of deceased persons. In practice, many of the sales which strictly require a sale by auction are now achieved by private treaty, subject to independent valuations and the approval of the Court since this saves considerable time and expense, but nevertheless mortgagees' sales by the Court are not infrequent.

A sale by auction by a seller who is free to choose his method of sale is effected by a Notary, who alone is competent to act as an auctioneer, through the *Marché Immobilier des Notaires*. To discover what is available at such sales, it is usually necessary to approach a Notary of one's choice for information. Such information will produce the properties on offer, the reserve prices, the amount of the deposit required to take part in the bidding, the times when the property may be visited and the name of the Notary acting for the seller. From the latter may be obtained information as to the planning situation, easements and other rights or burdens affecting the land, the costs and disbursements of the purchase and similar information such as one would seek on behalf of a client in England hoping to buy at auction.

To be entitled to take part in the auction, it is necessary to hand to the Notary acting for the seller a certified cheque for the deposit (which is returned to unlucky bidders) and information as to one's *état civil*.

Traditionally, the sales are 'candle auctions' that is to say a taper is used instead of the auctioneer's hammer. At the appropriate moment, two tapers are successively lit, each on extinction giving out a puff of smoke so that everyone can see clearly when this happens. It is the person who has made the highest bid immediately prior to the extinction of the second taper who is named as the buyer.

Completion normally is fixed for forty-five days after the sale but the sale does not become binding at the auction sale. In any event, it is subject to the usual rights of pre-emption but more curiously for a period of usually ten days after the auction (which will be notified in the pre-auction particulars) any person may make a higher bid than a new reserve which is usually 110% of the highest bid at the auction (*surenchère*) and oust the erstwhile purchaser, when a new period of forty-five days begins. In the event of the bidder who is finally the purchaser failing to complete, the seller has among other remedies the right to put the property up again for what is not surprisingly called a 'mad auction' or *folle enchere*.

The notarial fees which falls on a purchaser may be slightly more than those involved in a sale by private treaty. In the latter, the commission paid for negotiating a sale falls in most parts of France on the seller and will usually be of the order of 5% ex-TVA. In the case of an auction, the cost is 2% ex-TVA and, except in certain rare cases, this is shared equally between seller and buyer. Thus, the seller saves a considerable part of his costs but the buyer will usually pay more.

There may be an advantage to a purchase by auction in this manner for those who need mortgage finance. A purchaser at a notarial auction will obtain an automatic loan from Crédit Foncier de France equivalent to 60% of the purchase price. This may be raised to 80% if the purchaser's status merits it.

The auction sale by the Court does not much differ in

procedure from that described above. Details of such sales are sparsely publicized though usually they appear on the unfortunate building involved itself. Such sales are dealt with not by Notaries but by *avocats* at whose office all the usual pre-sale information may be obtained and to whom deposit cheques prior to auction are given. Sales take place in Court, frequently at strangely early hours and are also *à la bougie*. In this case, however, private bidders may not take part and all bids must be made through an *avocat* acting for a bidder. Auctions of this kind are generally noisy and somewhat confusing affairs.

Part II
Succession Law

16 Succession Law – Some General Principles

French succession law contains a number of points which are wholly at variance with the English law of succession. It is as well to have an overall appreciation of the more important differences which are dealt with in this chapter. To avoid repetition, certain aspects of the law are elaborated in subsequent chapters, to which reference should be made.

Article 3 of the Code Civil provides that 'Realty, even when owned by a foreigner, is governed by French law.' Notwithstanding the apparent clarity of intent of this Article, considerable inroads have in fact been made into the principle which it enunciates. The French Courts have over the years been content to deal with many commercial and marriage contracts involving interests in realty in accordance with the laws of other countries where either they have been chosen by the parties as the proper law or have been considered by the French Courts to be more appropriate than French law. They have nevertheless taken the view that the framers of the Code Civil intended this Article to embrace the previous rule of law that succession to realty was always governed by the law of the place where it was situate. Changing conditions over nearly two centuries have taken from the ownership of land the significance previously attached to it as a basic source of family wealth and cohesion and as an indication of social rank, which explains the insistence in pre-Code Civil days that land devolve according to the *lex situs*. Whilst the ownership of personal assets has now supplanted in significance the ownership of land, the Courts have firmly maintained the rule that French law governs the devolution on death of French land.

On the other hand, it is an established rule of French law that the devolution of personalty is governed by the law of the domicile at the date of death of the owner of that personalty.

It is certain that in some cases the effect of international conventions will appear to create inroads into these clear-cut rules and that it will not always be possible clearly to establish what is realty and what is personalty or where an asset is deemed to be situate but in most cases the rules hold good and serve as a safe guide.

At the time when the Code Civil was first promulgated, a foreigner could not share in the estate of a French citizen unless the law of that foreigner's country accorded reciprocal rights permitting French citizens to share in his estate. The rule remained in force for only a few years but on its repeal at a time when it seemed that not all countries in fact granted such reciprocity, a law retaining for French beneficiaries a certain measure of protection was enacted in its place. This law, still in force, provided that, in the case of the distribution of a French estate whose beneficiaries were both French and non-French and in which there were both French and non-French assets, the French beneficiaries had the prior right to a distribution out of French assets in an amount equal to their share in non-French assets, in which 'by local law or custom' they were prevented from sharing. The rule has somewhat surprisingly been judicially interpreted (although this interpretation is by no means without its critics) to mean that, whilst the law applies only for the benefit of persons French by nationality, it can take effect when all the beneficiaries are of French nationality. A mixture of French and foreign beneficiaries is not necessary, although the estate must consist of assets both in and outside France. It will hardly apply as between English and French beneficiaries in an estate with English and French assets but France is not the only country to feel the need still to impose such a rule. It exists in Belgium and a number of African and South American countries. The rule is known in French law as *le droit de prélèvement successoral*.

French textbooks on the law of succession tend to deal with gifts *inter vivos*, wills and intestacies as one subject or sometimes to divide them into gifts *inter vivos* and testamentary gifts (*liberalités*) on the one hand and intestacies on the other hand. The effect of the entrenched inheritance rights accorded to certain beneficiaries by French law, together with the consequent inter-relationship of gifts made by a deceased person during his lifetime and the distribution of his estate on his death, makes this inevitable.

The law which governs the devolution on death governs when and where the estate is administered and who qualify as beneficiaries and in what proportions. Thus, assuming that French succession law is applicable, French commorientes rules will normally apply and the circumstances necessary to ensure survival by a beneficiary so to entitle him to inherit is also a matter of French law. On the other hand, whilst French law decides the principles as to whether illegitimate or 'adulterine' children may inherit in an intestacy or be included among those who have entrenched inheritance rights and to what proportions they are entitled, it would appear that French law considers that it is the law of the domicile of the claimant beneficiary which decides whether he is in fact an adopted, illegitimate or 'adulterine' child of the deceased.

Articles 720 et seqq. of the Code Civil provide a most complex system of rules in the case of commorientes. These rules apply only if (a) evidence is not available to prove which of two or more persons was the first to die and (b) if the persons so dying are entitled respectively to share each in the estate of the other. In addition, for the Articles to apply, the deaths must result from the same event, which must be of a specific and not of a general nature. Thus, two deaths resulting from a single car or aircraft accident are within the scope of the rules. However, if two deaths result from (say) the same earthquake, the rules do not apply unless both persons were at the time together in the same house at the time it was destroyed; if they were killed by the same earthquake at the same time but in adjoining houses, the Articles would not apply. They are applicable (or, it is also said, are applied by the Courts) only to intestacies.

It is necessary to appreciate the position under French law of the Executor appointed under an English will by a domiciled English testator whose estate includes French property. From the view point of French law, if the administration of the estate is governed by English law, the former will recognize the power given by the latter, as the proper law of the succession, to call in, sell and distribute assets in France. In so far as personalty is concerned, there is no conflict between French and English law, since in respect of personalty a Testator may give 'ownership' (*saisine*) to his *exécuteur testamentaire* (see Chapter 17), and hence an English Executor acting under his powers in English Law can freely sell French personalty. But when it comes to realty, there is a total conflict since the concept of the English Executor is wholly at variance with French Law as to the devolution of realty (see Chapter 20) and to quote a leading French textbook 'recognition of the trust having regard to the present state of (French law) poses problems which are virtually insurmountable'. The current and seemingly correct line adopted by the Notary when faced with an English Will of a Testator owning realty in France is to accept the powers of sale of the Executor or Trustee but require all *héritiers réservataires* to join in the sale.

In many cases it is necessary to consider whether it is necessary for a Testator domiciled in England to make a French Will in respect of any French assets he may own. Usually, the nature of the assets in question provide the answer. No Will – French or English – is needed to pass property owned *en tontine* or which is subject to a *régime de communauté universelle*. If all that is owned in France is personalty, little is gained by having a French Will to deal only with such assets. It is far simpler to proceed under an English Will with Executors of whom there are probably not more than two or three than under a French Will where many if not all the beneficiaries may have to join in the administration. If residuary beneficiaries are charities, there is a clear advantage in proceeding under an English Will. Where there is a joint bank account in France, it will almost certainly be operable by the surviving account holder and from a practical point of view title to personal chattels will only very rarely require any formality to pass in France on the death of their owner unless they are to be sent out of the country. Ownership of a car registered in France may represent more of a problem but can frequently be dealt with at the *Préfecture* on the basis of a *certificat de coutume* proving devolution under English law in the form of the precedent contained in Appendix A.

As a very general rule, it is unlikely that a French Will is needed unless the Testator is domiciled in France or has substantial assets in that country and even then it is often a question of practical rather than legal circumstances which govern the issue. Among the practical circumstances involved is certainly the place in France where *la succession est ouverte* (see Chapter 20). It is suggested that if it is in a place where the local Notary sees few foreigners, there may be an advantage in allowing him to deal with a French Will, with which he will be familiar rather than with an English Probate with which he will certainly be unfamiliar. It must, of course, be remembered that any provision in an English Will in respect of French assets which offends against French law is liable to be overridden but there is no reason why an English Will should not be written in a form which, in respect of French assets, complies with French law.

Reference should be made to Appendix A for a note on the procedure to be adopted in France when French property passes under an English Will.

A separate French Will will normally be in French holograph form. It can be in English form and be written in English using English phraseology but this is undesirable. Anything other than a straightforward French Will is certain to cause unnecessary problems and expenses. It must be remembered that there is no Probate Registry in France in the sense in which it exists in England, so that the Notary, when dealing with the 'proof' of Wills, is virtually judge in his own cause and it is, in effect, left to the beneficiaries to take points which the Registry might take in England. As indicated above there is no merit in presenting a Notary with a linguistic and legal situation with which he is unfamiliar, bearing in mind that, from a practical point of view, in the case of an owner of French land dying domiciled and resident in England, the place where the French administration will take place is where the property is situate and many English owners buy in deep country.

No French Will should ever be executed without prior consultation with the testator's Solicitor in England so that, among other things, his English Will can be limited in scope to exclude French assets. It is also highly desirable that there be similar liaison where an English testator domiciled in

France has assets out of France where again, two Wills may be desirable. It must be remembered that the expression 'my testamentary expenses' does not include the payment of non-UK death duties. French death duties are payable by each beneficiary in respect of the assets he inherits and, from a practical point of view, often before he can physically lay his hands on them. On certain occasions, therefore, it may be desirable to extend the definition of testamentary expenses to include the payment of 'duties payable in France on or by reason of my death'. Beneficiaries who inherit land and immediately sell may apply the proceeds of sale in payment of duty and duty can, with suitable safeguards for the French Revenue, be paid by instalments.

Subsequent chapters deal with the making of French Wills, the order of distribution of intestate estates, entrenched inheritance rights and French administration procedure. Duties payable on death are dealt with in Chapter 22.

17 *Wills*

Articles 967 to 980 of the Code Civil deal with the making of Wills, of which in France there are three types. Article 968 forbids the making of joint Wills in one document whether in the form of a mutual Will or in favour of beneficiaries other than the Testators. In general terms, the equivalent of a covenant *inter vivos* to grant a benefit by Will is void.

The types of Wills available are:

1. *Le Testament Olographe.* Such a Will does not accord with the requirements of Article 970 of the Civil Code unless it is 'written in its entirety in the hand of and dated and signed by the Testator'. The Article adds that no other formalities are required. This is by far the most usual type of Will made by the French. Wording is on the whole far less technical than in an English Will. The words 'written in its entirety' may prove a trap for the English Testator and his English adviser, used as they are to the requirement of attesting witnesses. *Prima facie* the wording of the article is mandatory. In certain cases, the French Courts have admitted the validity of holograph Wills where the handwriting of a person other than the Testator appears provided that the words in such handwriting in no way affect the dispositions. It has, however, also been held that if handwriting other than the Testator's appears in a Will in order to comply with non-French requirements as to formal validity, e.g. two witnesses such as is required for English Wills, this will vitiate the Will. The only safe rule for English Testators therefore can be in any event to avoid the use of attesting witnesses, however strange this may be to them and ensure that none but the Testator's handwriting is used since otherwise their beneficiaries will inevitably become involved in a French Probate action.

2. *Le Testament Authentique.* This type of Will is in the form of a notarial document and is therefore a document of public record. Its advantage over the holograph Will is that the date of its execution and its contents (except as to their construction) cannot be questioned. Such a Will is made before two Notaries or one Notary and two witnesses. In either case, the contents are dictated by the Testator to the or one of the Notaries, who either writes it in his own handwriting or more usually causes it to be typed. It is then read over to the Testator, to which the document must contain specific reference. The Will is then signed by the Testator in the presence of the two Notaries or of one Notary and two witnesses.

3. *Le Testament Mystique.* A Will in this form is either a Will which fulfils the requirements of a holograph Will or is a Will written by a person other than the Testator at his direction. It is placed in an envelope sealed with sealing wax and the envelope is presented to a Notary in the presence of two witnesses or it may be closed and sealed in their presence. The Testator declares the document to be his Will, indicating whether it has been written by him or by another, and if by another, he confirms its terms. All these formalities are recited in a notarial document signed by the Testator, the officiating Notary and the two witnesses. Persons who are illiterate or are physically unable to read cannot make Wills of this type, and special provisions apply to Testators who can read but cannot speak.

In both the case of *le testament authentique* and of *le testament mystique*, no beneficiary under the Will nor any relation of such a beneficiary as distant as the fourth degree may be a witness, nor may a clerk of the Notary receiving the Will act as a witness. A witness must be a French citizen of full legal capacity and may be of either sex, but husband and wife cannot witness the same document.

Marriage does *per se* not revoke a Will. Divorce, on the other hand, may result in revocation. A decree of divorce or judicial separation granted on any of the grounds amounting to the wrongful behaviour of the respondent (as opposed to a divorce by consent) results in the automatic revocation of all provisions in any existing Will of the Petitioner in favour of the Respondent. If the decree is granted on the general ground of the breakdown of the marriage, there is automatic revocation of benefits in the Respondent's Will in favour of the Petitioner. In cases of 'consent' decrees, there is no automatic revocation of existing Wills, but it is common for suitable arrangements to be dealt with in the decree itself.

The English concept that a beneficiary who causes the death of the person under whose Will he benefits may be excluded from that benefit is wider in its effect under French law. The French Courts may revoke a benefit for 'ingratitude', and 'ingratitude' includes an attempt on the life of, the perpetration of acts of cruelty against or causing serious damage to the Testator, or causing serious injury to the memory of the Testator.

Revocation may be express or implied. Destruction of a Will by the Testator or by another on his instructions revokes a Will. Article 1035 deals with express revocation either in a subsequent Will or by a notarial document of revocation, which, as in the case of the *testament authentique*, requires either two notaries or one notary and two witnesses. Implied revocation is covered by Article 1036 of the Code Civil, which states that, 'Subsequent Wills which do not contain an express revocation of former Wills revoke only those dispositions contained in such former Wills as are incompatible or inconsistent with the latter.' Case law over a period of years has laid down that the decision whether subsequent dispositions are 'incompatible or inconsistent with' previous dispositions depends on evidence of the actual or presumed intentions of the Testator or the wording used by him or all the circumstances surrounding the case in issue.

The *Exécuteur Testamentaire* is under French law a wholly different creature from the English Executor. The assets of a French deceased person do not, except in the one case referred to below, vest in his Executor. Nine short Articles only of the Code Civil (Articles 1025-1034 (1029 is repealed)) deal with his duties and powers. The task of the *Exécuteur Testamentaire*, if one is indeed appointed, is a supervisory one limited to 'watching over' the carrying into effect of the terms of the Will. He can be given 'ownership' of the whole or part of the personalty comprised in the estate (not of realty) but such 'ownership' lasts only for a period of one year from the date of death. During that period he can dispose of assets in the nature of personalty in order to pay legacies if there is not sufficient cash. In the case of a dispute as to the validity of the Will, an Executor should join in any action to uphold the Will. He is required, at the end of the 'Executor's year', to account to the beneficiaries. An infant cannot be an Executor, and it is interesting to note that Article 1032 of the Code Civil specifically states that the powers of an *Exécuteur Testamentaire* do not pass to his heirs. The expenses incurred by an Executor in carrying out his duties are a charge against that part of the estate not included in the *réserve*.

Article 999 of the Code Civil provides that a Frenchman finding himself in a foreign country may make a holograph or Authentic Will 'in the form valid in the place where such document is made'. This Article has been interpreted by the French Courts in such a way as to provide reciprocity for the non-French Testator in France. Hence he may make testamentary dispositions which will be recognized by the French Courts as valid *in form* either by using one of the three types specified in the Code Civil or by executing a Will in a form valid according to the laws of his nationality. It must be emphasized that this gives him choice as to formal but not as to essential validity.

The Trust and all its conveniences are unknown to French law. Any provision which required a beneficiary to preserve and pass on (*à charge de conserver et rendre*) property to a third person is void in every respect (Article 896), so that the beneficiary of such a gift does not take absolutely free of the unlawful provision. Certain exceptions to this rule, however, permit *substitution fidéicommissaire*. These are:

1. The gift *inter vivos* or by Will of a life interest in property to one person and the reversion in that property to another is lawful. In this connection it must be remembered that such gifts do not involve the creation of a trust but life tenant and reversioner each have a 'legal estate' in the property. Hence, the life tenant has an interest in the property which he 'passes on' but there are special rules which deal with the rights and obligations as between life tenant and reversioner.

2. A parent may out of that part of his estate of which he may freely dispose, i.e. which is not subject to the entrenched

rules of succession (see Chapter 18), make a gift *inter vivos* or by Will to one or more of his children subject to the obligation *de conserver et rendre* such property for the benefit of such children's children but not remoter issue.

3. A Testator who dies without leaving issue may make a gift out of property and in circumstances similar to those in 2 above to brothers and sisters for the benefit of their children but not remoter issue.

4. In cases 2 and 3 above, any provision which is not for the benefit of all the children of a child or of a brother or sister (as the case may be), both in existence at the time when the gift takes effect and thereafter to be born and irrespective of their sex or age is void.

5. A curious provision contained in Article 1051 of the Code Civil permits a derogation from the rule that children only but not more remote issue of the donee or legatee subject to the obligation *de conserver et rendre* may benefit from *substitution fidéicommissionaire*. If such a donee or legatee dies leaving no children surviving, even if such predeceased children themselves had children, such surviving grandchildren take no benefit and the *substitution* falls to the ground. However, if he dies leaving at least one child surviving and the children of other children who had predeceased him also surviving, the surviving child and the surviving grandchildren all benefit from the arrangement.

6. The law limits the extent to which a donee or legatee may deal with the property subject to the *substitution* so as not to compromise its subsequent devolution. The Donor or Testator may widen these limits and may also nominate a *Tuteur*, whose task is not to behave as a trustee and administer the property in question himself but to ensure its proper administration by the donee or legatee. If such a person is not appointed by the Donor or Testator or if for some reason he does not or cannot accept this office, the donee or legatee must within one month of whichever is the earlier of (i) the death of the donor or testator or (ii) the coming to light of the document creating the *substitution* appoint such a *Tuteur*. If he fails to do this, the Court may on the application of the reversioners or of its own volition determine the interest of the defaulting donee or legatee so that immediate possession of the property free of his interest is vested in the reversioners.

France has not yet created by law the system of compulsory registration of Wills envisaged by the Convention signed in Basle by the then Members of the EEC on 16 May 1972 and ratified by France on 6 May 1976. Pending the necessary legislation, the governing body of the Notarial profession (*le Conseil Supérieur du Notariat*) has set up a central register of Wills at 17, chemin des Tamaris, 13100, Aix-en-Provence. Notaries who have drawn *testaments authentiques* or codicils or documents of revocation in authentic form, or to whom safe custody of such documents or of *testaments olographes* or *mystiques* has been given, will register such documents at that central registry subject, in the case of the two latter types of Wills, to the consent of the Testator. Registration of the removal from the custody of a Notary of such Wills is obligatory.

18 Entrenched Succession Rights

Of all the rules of French succession law most likely to surprise the English practitioner it is those dealing with the entrenched inheritance rights given to certain members of the family. The rules will, of course, apply to every English domiciled owner of realty in France and to the assets, both real and personal wherever they may be situate, of the English owner domiciled in France. It is no more surprising that the French Notary is often unaware that the rules of succession which he applies every day do not run in England than is it that the English adviser is not conversant with those rules. How their effect may in suitable circumstances be circumvented is dealt with elsewhere (see Chapter 19); suffice it to say here that use of an English Will to devise French realty will not *per se* achieve this. Those who have seen the effect of the rules upon unsuspecting and improperly advised English owners, their surviving spouses and families will not need warning twice.

Articles 913 and 914 of the Code Civil impose limits upon how much by way of gift, be the gift *inter vivos* or testamentary, a person may freely dispose of without encroaching upon the rights given to ascendants and descendants in the direct line to inherit predetermined parts of a deceased's estate. The part which is destined for these members of a family is called the *réserve légale*, and the persons so entitled are *héritiers réservataires*. A surviving spouse *has no such rights* in a testate succession, it being left to the Testator entirely to decide whether he wishes to make provision (as indeed he may) by varying to some extent the nature of the interests of ascendants and/or descendants in order to give something to the surviving spouse.

Briefly the rules are set out below:

1. If the deceased has one child, that child is entitled to one half of his parent's estate; if he has two children, those children are together entitled to two-thirds of the estate; if there are three or more children, they share equally in three-quarters of the estate.

2. Issue of deceased children take by representation *per stirpes* their deceased parent's share.

3. Children who are adopted under the 'full' adoption procedure, which has an effect more or less equivalent to an English adoption, are treated for all purposes of succession as legitimate children of the adopting parents but children who are adopted under the 'simple' procedure, which is unknown to English law, have the rights of a legitimate child of the adopting parents only but no rights in estates of other members of that family e.g. as grandchildren of their parents' parents. Illegitimate children also count for this purpose as legitimate children but if they are 'adulterine', their share may in certain circumstances be reduced.

4. Provided that there are no descendants, ascendants are *héritiers réservataires*. If ascendants in both lines are living, each line benefits from one quarter of the estate; if members of one line only are alive, that line is entitled to one quarter. As with children, there is no limit to representation backwards i.e. living grandparents would take in the place of deceased parents.

5. Article 1094 of the Code Civil makes the following provisions:

(i) If the Testator leaves children, the surviving spouse may (a) benefit from that part of the estate which the Testator may freely dispose of or (b) take one quarter of the estate absolutely and enjoy a life interest in the other three quarters or (c) have a life interest in the whole estate. The Testator may himself make the choice in his Will or may delegate by Will the choice to the surviving spouse.

(ii) If the Testator leaves *only* 'adulterine' children surviving, the surviving spouse is then entitled under Article 1097 of the Code Civil to either (a) three-quarters of the estate absolutely or (b) one half of the estate absolutely and a life interest in the other half or (c) a life interest in the whole of the estate. Again, the surviving spouse may be left the choice or the Testator may make it himself in his Will. This method of distribution does not apply if only some of the surviving children are 'adulterine'.

(iii) If the Testator leaves ascendants but no issue, a surviving spouse may be given, in addition to such part of the estate as is not reserved for ascendants, the reversion to that part destined for the ascendants, thus reducing those persons' interests from absolute interests to mere life interests.

(iv) In certain circumstances, children (but not 'adulterine' children) of the deceased or their issue by representation may each in respect of his own share in reversion require that the life interest given to the surviving spouse be converted into an annuity (*rente viagère*) suitably secured and, if necessary, indexed. If this is not done, the reversioners are entitled to the same protection in respect of what is to all intents and purposes a settled fund as is given in the case of the creation of a *substitution fidéicommissaire* (see Chapter 17). Children of the Testator by one or more marriages previous to that subsisting at the date of his death may, subject to specific directions in the Will to the contrary, to some extent reduce the nature of the interest given to a surviving spouse.

In connection with the failure of the Code Civil to include a surviving spouse as an *héritier réservataire*, it must be remembered that every French married couple has a *régime matrimonial* either by choice or in default by operation of law. Thus, in the case of a husband and wife married under the *régime* of *communauté de biens*, the surviving spouse continues to be the owner of his or her half of the *communauté*, irrespective of whether he or she has benefited by way of gift *inter vivos* or from the Will of the deceased spouse. The French are noticeably conscious of property rights and it is safe to assume that the parties to a marriage (or more probably their parents) will have carefully considered which of the various *régimes matrimoniaux* should apply to them, having regard to a variety of circumstances of which the rule as to surviving spouses is but one.

It is always possible for children or ascendants to renounce their rights but the procedure is slightly tedious and there will be considerable difficulties if, for example, there are any children who are not *sui juris* (see Chapter 20). Moreover, it is not easy or in many cases proper to persuade a child out of what is its lawful right merely because one of its parents was not adequately advised, particularly when proper methods do exist to defeat such a child's right if a parent had wanted to use them.

Although the rules which govern the effect of gifts *inter vivos* made by a deceased donor on the distribution of his estate apply whether there is a *réserve legale* in the estate or not, it is convenient to consider them in this chapter because of the results which flow from the existence of a *réserve* in an estate.

Gifts *inter vivos* may be made either on the basis that they are subject to being brought into hotchpot or relieved therefrom. Article 843 of the Code Civil stipulates that gifts are deemed to be subject to hotchpot unless the contrary intention is stated by the donor. Gifts may, therefore, be either *par avancement d'hoirie*, which is a straightforward advance subject to hotchpot, or *par préciput et hors part*, which prima facie frees the gift from being brought into hotchpot. There are, of course, no rules such as bind English Trustees as to what is a proper advancement, since the donor is always an absolute owner. Parents will make the usual gifts, such as the setting up in business of a son or the providing of a dowry for a daughter and certain advancements are, notwithstanding that they are not expressed to be *par préciput*, free from hotchpot. These include the cost of maintaining and educating children, the normal expenses of a marriage and wedding presents and the payment by a deceased donor of premiums on policies on his life effected for the benefit of a beneficiary in his estate provided that the cost of the premiums is reasonable relative to the deceased's financial position. A beneficiary who renounces his interest under a Will is not required to bring into hotchpot (or, more strictly in such a case, to repay) gifts made to him by the deceased unless there are *héritiers réservataires* who would go short if such repayment in whole or in part were not made.

It is precisely this point which complicates the effect of gifts made *par préciput*. Gifts which have been made by a deceased donor, be they free of or subject to hotchpot, can, in the eventual reckoning, only be made out of that part of his estate of which he can freely dispose. It is evident that the *réserve* on the one hand and the freely disposable balance on the other can only be ascertained immediately after the death of the donor. It may then be found *ex post facto* that the deceased donor has in making his gifts exceeded the total of that part of his estate not subject to the *réserve*.

It is not considered that French law relating to gifts forms part of the subject matter of this book except to the extent that gifts impinge on the manner in which estates come to be distributed. To the extent that there may be fiscal advantages in making *inter vivos* gifts, it seems very unlikely that non-French domiciled owners of French assets will make gifts out of those assets. The most careful advice would be required if such a course of action were envisaged and it would be essential that the advice obtained were on the effect of such a gift in both French and English law. It is, however, interesting to note some of the provisions of French law relating to gifts.

1. Certain formalities attendant upon the making of a gift must be complied with to avoid the gift being void. It must, save in the case of gifts where possession can pass by manual delivery, be made by notarial *acte*. Apart from obvious objects such as jewellery or furniture, it has been held that bearer securities, stock in trade and sometimes cheques do not require an *acte notarié*. Proof of such a gift in cases, for example, where beneficiaries seek to force another beneficiary to bring it into hotchpot must normally be supported or at least initiated by writing if the value of the gift exceeds 5,000 francs.

2. Acceptance of the gift must be formal and recorded in the *acte*.

3. In the case of a gift of personalty, a full inventory with values must be prepared.

4. The *acte de donation* must be registered at the *bureau des hypothèques*.

5. A Donor may include in the *acte de donation* a provision under which, in the event of (i) the donee or (ii) the donee and his issue predeceasing the donor, the subject matter of the gift becomes retransferable to the donor. This provision is known as the *retour conventionnel*.

6. Gifts are generally irrevocable. However, if certain

obligations which go to the root of the gift are imposed on the donee and he fails to fulfil them, the Court has a discretion to revoke the gift. The gift is also revocable if the donee (i) makes an attempt on the life of the donor, (ii) behaves physically towards the donor in an outrageous manner or is guilty of a tort or crime against the donor or (iii) refuses to supply him with necessaries leaving him in want. Gifts between spouses made during marriage are freely revocable.

19 Avoidance of Entrenched Succession Rights

Few, if any, rules of French law are likely to give such concern to English buyers of land in France and their advisers as those relating to the succession to property. The Code Civil clearly intends that its Articles in this respect should always apply and social pressures still favour their maintenance. However, there can be no reason for the English owner of French property to submit to them, alien as they are to the English way of life, if they can with propriety be circumvented – avoidance as opposed to evasion in a non-fiscal sphere.

Chapter 10 deals with the possibility of avoiding the *réserve* rules by the use of companies as owners to turn realty into personalty but on many occasions this involves expense disproportionate to the value of the property and even if this is not so, this solution may be quite unnecessarily cumbersome. There remain at least two considerably less expensive alternatives of which one is the use of the *tontine*. This chapter seeks to develop the reasoning behind this alternative. It is not intended to be exhaustive of the subject and no decisions based on its contents should be taken without due consideration of the facts of each case and the fullest advice. It is urged that such advice should not be limited to that of the Notary involved in the relevant purchase (for whomever he may act) but that the views of a lawyer with a good working knowledge of both English and French law should be sought.

As has been explained in Chapter 9, ownership *en tontine* may be taken as the equivalent of English joint tenancy. Such joint ownership results, as under English law, in the whole of the property passing automatically to the survivor on the death of the first joint owner. There are a number of reasons why on a purchase by English owners the average Notary will assume in the absence of instructions that the joint ownership is to be *en indivision*. Even if purchasers are quite clear in their instructions, the pressure which can be applied against the use of the *tontine* can be considerable. It is therefore necessary to appreciate what is behind this pressure in order to resist it successfully. Let there be no mistake, as an article by a member of the Bar of one of the French Appeal Courts has said '*Le pacte tontinier est à la mode*' but remarkably few Notaries seem to have caught up with the '*mode*'.

1. Until 1980, there was a tax advantage in the use of the *tontine* which no longer applies. Previously, the argument was that since joint ownership *en tontine* was of the nature explained in Chapter 9, on the death of the first joint owner to die what passed was by way of a transfer for full value and was not in the nature of a gift. This view, taken by the Courts over a number of years was not attractive to the French Revenue since a transfer for value involved stamp duty of about 8% *ad valorem* whilst a gift can produce *droits de succession* of anything up to 60%. The Finance Law 1980 finally overrode the *Cour de Cassation* and death duties (subject to the very important exception mentioned in Chapter 22) are now payable on the death of one co-owner at the appropriate rate on half the value of the property. Hence, the Notary takes the view that since there is now no fiscal advantage in using the *tontine*, there is no need to use it.

2. It must be remembered that few Notaries appreciate that in England, Inheritance Tax is prima facie payable on half the value of jointly owned property whatever the method of joint ownership may be, so that the present French law represents nothing unusual for English owners. Equally, he knows nothing of English surviving spouse exemption so that, all in all, fiscally the Notary approaches the problem for the English buyer from a totally wrong angle.

3. The other aspect of a *tontine* purchase present in the mind of a Notary is the possibility based on the provisions of Article 1099 of the Code Civil that it may be upset by the *héritiers réservataires*. This Article reads as follows: 'One party to a marriage may not transfer by way of gift to the

other amounts in excess of that permitted by the provisions hereinbefore contained (i.e. the *réserve* rules) and any such gift whether disguised or made through a third party shall be void'. The best interpretation of this Article seems to be that all such gifts are void *in toto* and not only as to that proportion which exceeds the amount of which a donor may freely dispose. How in the case of a purchase *en tontine* does Article 1099 apply in the event that it is one spouse who pays the purchase price entirely out of his own pocket but has the property transferred to himself and his wife jointly with the provision that on the death of the first to die, the *réserve* rules do not apply?

Recent Court of Appeal judgments show that it is extremely difficult if not wellnigh impossible for *héritiers réservataires* to substantiate a claim that a purchase *en tontine* is in breach of this Article. To succeed in such a claim in effect requires proof that one of the parties could not in any circumstances have had the funds at the date of purchase to have provided his or her share and it is considered that such proof is almost impossible to adduce. It is interesting to note that a statement in the *acte de vente* on a purchase *en tontine* that the funds came from both purchasers may well, in the opinion of the Court of Appeal, be incontrovertible and the Notary preparing the *acte* cannot enquire into the genuineness of such a statement. In reliance on this opinion, the Power of Attorney for a purchase contained in Appendix A refers to the source of the funds as should the purchase document itself.

Moreover, even if against all the odds, heirs succeed in overturning an *en tontine* purchase on the grounds that the transaction was a disguised or indirect gift, the property in question is not reintegrated into the estate of the deceased co-owner. All that will be recoverable will be the value in cash at the date of death of the gift.

There exists a further alternative to the use of the *tontine* to circumvent the application of the *réserve*. This alternative which involves the use of one of the French *régimes matrimoniaux* is usually available to English buyers because English couples are not subject to the burdens of marriage contracts from the outset of their marriage. However, this alternative is one which requires the most careful advice from those well versed not only in French domestic law but also French and English Private International Law and should *never* be adopted without such advice. It suffers from the disadvantage that a child of a *former* but not the current marraige of the first joint owner to die may apply to the Court for a declaration that the adoption of this method of ownership by his parent is void to the extent that it has deprived the applicant of his rights as *héritier réservataire*. Although there may not be many instances where this disadvantage is in issue, if it is, there is no possibility of avoiding its impact since the reasoning behind the judgments in the *tontine* cases does not apply and it is impossible for a child to renounce in advance of his parent's death his rights under the relevant article of the Code Civil.

From a fiscal point of view, the two methods produce interestingly different results. In the case of a purchase *en tontine*, with the exception only of the case referred to in Chapter 22, French Inheritance Tax is payable on the death of the first co-owner to die on half the then value of the property. The rate will depend on the relationship of deceased co-owner to surviving co-owner, which usually will be that of husband and wife. The rates and thresholds are shown in Appendix B. On the other hand, on the death of a spouse in respect of property held in the further alternative manner, no *droits de succession* are payable and stamp duty at approximately 8% only is charged.

Thus the following factors should govern the decision how a purchase should be made by joint owners.

1. A purchase *en tontine* can be made by any two or more persons irrespective of their relationship. Only married couples can use the other alternative.

2. The fiscal advantages of the latter method of purchase increase fairly steeply as the value of the property increases unless the property ranks for the *en tontine* exemption. This may arise when the property in question is worth 500,000 francs or less.

3. If there are only children of the existing marriage of the co-owners, on balance only the *droit de succession* situation is involved.

4. If there are children of a marriage prior to that of the co-owners, it may be safer to eschew the alternative to the *tontine* purchase unless the party to the marriage who has such children is more likely to be the first to die.

20 The Administration of Estates

No steps in the administration of an estate in France can begin until a Death Certificate has been obtained, since a Notary will require production of this document before he can take any procedural steps.

When dealing with probate matters, English practitioners must disabuse themselves of the fairly obvious notion that few, if any, persons would instruct a Solicitor to obtain a Grant of Representation to the estate of a person yet alive. It comes absolutely naturally to the French client that the first thing he has to do when instructing a Notary to deal with the administration of an estate is to put a Death Certificate on the table. It is a reverence for *état civil* and the written word, fostered assiduously by *l'administration*, which accounts for this attitude to be found in every dealing with the French. Strangely enough, the Birth Certificate (or possibly passport) of a foreign deceased will also often be asked for, particularly if there is a sale of property involved, since the *enregistrement* apparently cannot believe without proof positive that a person who has died was born.

Notice of death must be given within twenty-four hours to the Registrar (*officier de l'état civil*) at the local Town Hall. Normally notice is given by a relative but may be given by anyone. In every case, as the standard guide has it, whoever gives notice must have available at that time 'the most exact and the most complete' information on the *état civil* of the deceased. Ideally, the declarant takes with him the deceased's *livret de famille*, his birth certificate and his identity card. Thus, in France, does officialdom follow one to the grave. An *acte de décès* is prepared, containing rather more information than is to be found in an English Death Certificate but no cause of death. There exists a special form of certificate in a number of languages which is sometimes used for the death of foreigners but, whilst it will be available in large cities and tourist centres, it will not easily be found in villages in the deep country. In the case of foreigners whose bodies are to be taken out of France the cause of death, which is normally required by the carrier and by the country to which it is going, can be obtained without difficulty. For burial in France, a further certificate is issued after the *acte de décès* on a doctor's subsequent certificate verifying death. Further certificates are necessary for cremation, now reasonably common in France.

Copies of *actes de décès* can always be obtained free of charge from the *mairie* where the death was registered. Although it seems unlikely that alterations would be made to a death certificate – and certainly not many years after a death, an *acte de décès* which has been bespoken no matter how long after the death but more than three months before the date on which it is to be used as evidence of that death is unacceptable. Hence the problem with English certificates referred to in the Glossary.

The whole administration of an estate in France is coloured for the English observer by the lack of the 'Personal Representative'. To quote a French handbook for the intelligent layman: 'From the moment administration commences (*la succession est ouverte*) the heir must look after his own interests' and that is precisely the situation. If there are several beneficiaries, they must get together and either all agree to instruct the same Notary or some must instruct one and some another. In some cases, of course, the deceased will have made a Will in notarial form, so the beneficiaries are immediately known to the family Notary. In probably many more cases, if a Will was made, it was in holograph form and was almost certainly kept at home. Banks will not normally keep documents for safe custody; Wills can be kept in safe deposit boxes, but these tend to become blocked on death with the Wills inside them. Holograph Wills, the execution of which requires no witnesses, kept at home can easily disappear and do easily disappear, and the family quarrel caused by a death and the distribution of an estate is a common tradition in France.

It is said that the English public complains at the time it takes the lawyers and professional Executors such as Banks to complete the administration of estates; in a few cases the complaint will be justified. In the administration of estates in France, everything combines to ensure delay in every case – from the legal system itself, with the lack of Personal Representative but the presence of a number of beneficiaries all entitled 'to administer' to the difficulties encountered in obtaining the kind of information or assistance or even replies to letters from all the authorities and individuals one requires to have contact with in the administration of an estate. There seems also to be another tradition – that all probate files go to the bottom of the basket and perhaps one should not blame the Notary overmuch, beset as he often will be by a number of squabbling beneficiaries, any one of whom can, by refusing to co-operate, cause untold delay. The atmosphere is totally different from that which prevails in England.

There is one further tradition which dogs the administration of estates in France. When taxation becomes burdensome, evasion begins. Not only are death duties in France relatively high, especially where those who inherit are even as close as brothers and sisters but death presents an excellent moment for assets to disappear – and disappear they do. Unfortunately it is not only the French Revenue which loses out: it is frequently the beneficiaries. The French are not a nation of investors in quoted registered shares or in any asset which requires any kind of open formality to acquire or dispose of. The bar of gold, cash, jewellery, bearer shares are all assets beloved of by the French in every walk of life. Suffice it to say that at least one real cause for delay in completing the administration of estates in France can be traced to the Revenue's efforts to catch disappearing assets, which are not conspicuously successful.

The services of a Notary are not obligatory in the administration of an estate but, since virtually every document which will be required is a notarial document, the Notary and his advice are normally essential. If a Will has been found in the form of a holograph or *mystique* Will, it must be handed to a Notary (Article 1007 of the Code Civil). The Notary will open the Will and prepare a record of its opening and condition which will be retained by him in his official records. Within one month thereafter, the Notary must send a certified copy of that document and of the Will to the Registrar of the *Tribunal de Grande Instance* for the area in which the administration will take place. Within three months of death, every Will must be produced to the *enregistrement*. In the case of a notarial Will, a copy must also be sent to the Court and filed with the *enregistrement*.

In the case of a testate succession, the property of a deceased person frequently passes directly to the appropriate beneficiary at the moment of death who acquires title (*la saisine*) without the need to become involved in any formalities or application to the Court. In the case of intestacies, all the persons entitled to share in the intestate's estate so acquire *saisine*. The State alone in the case of *bona vacantia* is not treated in this way.

Héritiers réservataires always obtain automatic *saisine*, whichever of the three types of Will is involved. Where the deceased has left a Will in notarial form and if there are no *héritiers réservataires*, the *légataire universel* obtains *saisine* on the Testator's death. If there are *héritiers réservataires*, it is they who formally transfer title (*délivrance du legs*) in respect of the assets he has inherited to the *légataire universel*.

If the Will is in holograph or *mystique* form and there are no *héritiers réservataires, légataires universels* must produce to the Court the notarial document referred to below and obtain a formal order (*l'envoi en possession*) conferring title on them.

The *légataire à titre universel* and the specific legatee must obtain from the *légataire universel* their respective formal *délivrance du legs*.

A feature of the French administration is the sealing of the deceased's premises (*apposition des scellés*). This formality may be requested of the local Court by, among others, the surviving spouse, any person claiming to have an interest in the estate, any *exécuteur testamentaire* appointed by the Will, the owner of the property in which the deceased lived, certain creditors, the local Mayor or a senior Police Officer or certain 'public' officers. The seals may be removed at the request of any of the above persons but unlawfully to remove the seals is a heinous crime with a suitable punishment. It is difficult to list circumstances in which premises may be sealed but it would be typical to find this done to premises owned by a foreigner with no immediately traceable family or contacts in France. Once the seals have been placed on the doors, the local Registrar (*Greffier*) will patiently wait until someone turns up with authority to act in the estate. This will frequently be a Notary duly instructed but on more than one occasion a *certificat de coutume* in suitable terms has opened up premises to appropriately qualified visiting representatives of English Executors. The object of this procedure is to protect the goods of the deceased against removal by the beneficiary who obtained *saisine* on the death of the deceased where some of these may be bequeathed elsewhere, and not against the predatory world at large.

The primary document prepared by the Notary engaged in the administration is the *acte de notoriété après décès* which, together with the *intitulé d'inventaire*, sets out the assets and liabilities of the estate as then known and the title of each beneficiary to the assets. In addition, if there is land involved in the estate, there must be prepared and filed within the time limits prescribed at the appropriate *bureau des hypothèques* an *attestation notariale immobilière* which, as a document of title, has much the same effect as an Assent by Executors. The object of its registration is, however, primarily fiscal, to keep the Cadastre up to date rather than to complete title. In the case of other assets, *certificats de propriété* will be necessary in order, for example, to enable the sale of securities or their transfer to a beneficiary; it is frequently this document which is provided from France where an English Grant is needed to deal with a domiciled Frenchman's assets in England.

No one, according to Article 775 of the Code Civil, is obliged to accept the inheritance which has fallen to him. Hence, a beneficiary may (i) accept unconditionally his interest under a Will or intestacy or (ii) accept it *sous bénéfice d'inventaire* or (iii) renounce his interest. The alternative chosen by a beneficiary is intended to reflect his views upon the present and future solvency of the estate but this does not mean that a renunciation may not be made for motives of generosity. A beneficiary who takes with automatic *saisine* may nevertheless renounce or accept *sous bénéfice d'inventaire* in the same manner as other beneficiaries, provided he does nothing prior to making such a decision which is deemed to be evidence of unconditional acceptance of the kind referred to below.

French law takes the view that capacity to exercise the

choice given to a beneficiary to accept or renounce a benefit under an intestacy or Will is governed by the law of the nationality of that beneficiary. The laws of England make no distinction as does the Code Civil between the 'emancipated infant' (i.e. a child who has married under the age of eighteen or has been 'emancipated' at an earlier age by the Court at the request of one or both of his or her parents) and a 'non-emancipated infant'. Whilst there is no problem if a boy or girl of eighteen or more needs to choose the method of acceptance of a benefit or wishes to renounce, procedural difficulties will certainly arise if a 'non-emancipated' infant or, indeed, any person having attained his majority but under some form of disability is involved.

A beneficiary has three months plus forty days in which to make his decision. The first period of three months, which runs from the date of the *ouverture de la succession*, allows for an account to be taken of the assets and liabilities of the estate. At the end of that period or from the date of the completion of the account, whichever is the earlier, the beneficiary has forty days in which to study the figures and accept in either of the two ways open to him or renounce. The period of forty days may be extended by the Court. During the period no third party may take any steps of a nature which might force the beneficiary to a decision. After the end of the period, if a beneficiary has still not reached a decision, he may be ordered to do so by the Court and on failure to comply with such an Order he will be adjudged to have accepted unconditionally. The period of prescription is thirty years, so that, in the unlikely event of the matter being left open for so long a time, at the end of that period the beneficiary who has not made his choice is deemed to have renounced.

Unconditional acceptance normally requires the completion of no formality. Once given, it is irrevocable and the beneficiary can no longer opt to renounce or accept *sous bénéfice d'inventaire*. Such acceptance can be express, i.e. by writing in any form by which the beneficiary indicates his unequivocal acceptance of the bequest. Hence, a hesitating beneficiary should be guarded in his correspondence. Acceptance can be tacit that is to say by some act on his part indicative of his intention to accept and which he could do only in his capacity of a beneficiary. The following have been held to involve tacit acceptance: the sale to a third party of an asset in the estate, the receipt of estate income, the removal of the deceased's effects before an inventory of them has been prepared or the recovery of a debt due to the estate. Finally, acceptance can be forced on a beneficiary in the case of *recel*. This is the crime of converting to one's own use or the fraudulent secreting of an asset in an estate to the detriment of other beneficiaries, for which the penalty is twofold. The perpetrator is deprived of his right to opt for acceptance or renunciation of his benefit in the estate, and he is deemed to have accepted unconditionally. He is also deprived of all rights in the asset in question.

Acceptance sous bénéfice d'inventaire involves certain formalities, primarily that of the beneficiary making a declaration before the Registrar of the local *Tribunal de Grande Instance* indicating his acceptance only *sous bénéfice d'inventaire*. To be effective, this declaration must be preceded or followed by the making of a full and true inventory of all the assets of the deceased by a Notary of the choice of the declarant. Any one individual beneficiary may accept in this way, and unanimity in the types of acceptance is not required from all the beneficiaries. It is unlawful for a testator to forbid a beneficiary to accept his bequest in this manner. Acceptance *sous bénéfice d'inventaire* may be made only by a beneficiary who has not and has not been deemed to have accepted unconditionally. Acceptance in this manner prevents subsequent renunciation but not subsequent unconditional acceptance. A beneficiary accepting in this manner who is guilty of *recel* or who wilfully or in bad faith causes assets to be omitted from the inventory referred to above is not allowed to accept *sous bénéfice d'inventaire*.

The beneficiary accepting unconditionally is liable without limit (jointly with other beneficiaries also so liable) for all the debts of the deceased and for all specific legacies made by the Will, even if this involves payment out of the beneficiaries own pocket. The beneficiary who accepts *sous bénéfice d'inventaire* is liable for the debts of the deceased to the extent only of the assets in the estate. For this reason, special rules govern the administration of an estate where the beneficiary or beneficiaries have accepted *sous bénéfice d'inventaire*.

Such a beneficiary is treated as the administrator of the estate. He is required to provide for the benefit of, among others, the creditors of the estate accounts relating to his management of the estate and may lose the protection of this method of acceptance if he fails to do so. He may sell personal effects only at public auction by a *commisseur-priseur*. As to realty and other assets, any sale should be effected with the greatest care and in conformity with certain rules as though the seller were not *sui juris*. If creditors or other interested parties so require, the beneficiary must provide suitable surety to cover the value of the personal assets and real assets (or of their equity of redemption, if charged) in the estate. Even after final approval of the accounts and the payment of all known creditors, if there remain any distributable assets in the estate, they stand charged for the benefit of creditors who have not yet 'proved' until such time as any such claims become barred. Hence the rules which apply to sales of assets during the administration proper apply also to assets in this distributable balance.

It must, however, be remembered that death duties in France are the personal liability of each of the beneficiaries and that liability is in no way affected by an *acceptation sous bénéfice d'inventaire*. It is generally considered that the amount of duty payable may figure on the debit side of the *inventaire* referred to above but, for reasons beyond the scope of this chapter, the amount which may so appear may in certain circumstances be considerably less than the amount actually paid.

Renunciation produces some curious results. In order to be effective not only as between the beneficiaries in the estate in which a benefit has been renounced but as between the renouncing beneficiary and third parties, renunciation must be by declaration made before the Registrar of the local *Tribunal de Grande Instance*, who records it in a special register. This formality can be effected through an Attorney. A beneficiary who renounces is freed from any obligation to bring into hotchpot any *advances d'hoirie* made to him *inter vivos* by the deceased so that it may become a question of pure mathematics whether to accept or renounce. The only exception is that, where there are *héritiers réservataires* and the effect of applying the rule would be to diminish the *réserve* because the advances exceed the *quotité disponible*, the renouncing beneficiary is liable to refund the appropriate part of his advance.

Creditors of a renouncing beneficiaries may apply to the Court for an order authorizing them to accept the renounced benefit in lieu of the renouncing beneficiary. Such an Order annuls the renunciation in favour of the creditors to the extent of the debts due to them but otherwise the renunciation remains fully effective.

A beneficiary may retract his renunciation provided that (a) his right of choice to accept or renounce has not become barred by prescription, (b) no other beneficiary has accepted the benefit which he has renounced and (c) such retraction would not prejudice rights acquired by third parties in the estate consequent upon his renunciation.

The method of distribution of an estate in France, other than to the specific legatees, suffers, as does almost every step in its general administration, from the lack of Personal Representatives. Unless there is only one residuary beneficiary, the alternatives are that either the beneficiaries other than specific legatees will remain *en indivision* (see Chapter 9) or there will be a *partage* or partition of the distributable assets to put an end to the state of *indivision*.

There is much law on *partages*, but it is unlikely that the problems with which the relevant Articles of the Code Civil are designed to cope will cause much difficulty to the English beneficiaries of French assets under the Will of an English testator. Suffice it therefore to say that *le partage* comes in four forms: (i) partial, which is self-explanatory (ii) provisional, that is to say, an ad hoc arrangement between beneficiaries pending a final distribution (iii) by consent, which is again self-explanatory and much to be desired and (iv) by the Court, which indicates usually but not necessarily, disagreement between the beneficiaries, for the aid of the Court must be sought also if one or more of the beneficiaries is for some reason absent and unrepresented or if there are beneficiaries who are not *sui juris*.

No one recommends intervention by the Court if this can possibly be avoided, if only because of the inordinate delay and expense involved and because in the last resort the distribution may take place by the drawing of lots. In such a case, the following assets (among many others) are treated specially, so that:

(i) *souvenirs de famille*, such as decorations, family portraits, letters and diplomas which have sentimental rather than monetary value, are distributed in the entire discretion of the Court;

(ii) the family tomb (which is far more common in France than in England) is not distributed by lot, nor is a 'judgment of Solomon' resorted to. It is handed over to blood relatives of the deceased even if they are not beneficiaries under the Will itself;

(iii) the lease of the deceased's home may benefit from a special method of distribution at the discretion of the Court if circumstances call for it. In any event, in the case of a surviving spouse, Article 1751 of the Code Civil provides that the lease of the matrimonial home, provided it has no professional or commercial user, irrespective of the *régime matrimonial* of the couple and notwithstanding any provision to the contrary and whether granted before or after the marriage, is deemed to belong to both spouses. Hence, on the death of one spouse, that lease belongs personally to the survivor.

21   Distribution on Intestacy

In order to qualify as a person entitled to share in a French intestacy, three conditions must be fulfilled. He must:

(i) in accordance with Article 725 of the Code Civil, be in existence at the moment of death of the intestate. Persons *en ventre sa mère* are not treated as being in existence unless they were conceived prior to the date of death of the intestate and were thereafter born alive with such physiological characteristics as are necessary to maintain life. The law deems a person so born less than 300 days after the death of the intestate to have fulfilled this condition:

(ii) be one of the persons designated by law so to share;

(iii) not be subject to any of the 'indignities' as defined by Articles 727 of the Code Civil which prevent a person otherwise qualified from sharing in an intestacy, viz: (a) to have been found guilty of murder or attempted murder of the deceased (b) to have defamed the deceased by falsely accusing him of a 'capital' crime or (c) being of full age, to have been privy to the murder of the deceased and to have failed to have notified the authorities.

The order of distribution in an intestacy is as follows:

i.   children and issue of the deceased
ii. brothers and sisters of the deceased and the surviving mother and the father of the deceased
iii. other ascendants of the deceased
iv. the surviving spouse of the deceased
v.   collateral relatives of the deceased, i.e. uncles, aunts and their issue
vi. the State

Article 745 of the Code Civil provides for surviving children and issue of the intestate to take to the entire exclusion of all others. No distinction is made between legitimate and illegitimate children. Children take equally, the issue of children who predecease the deceased taking *per stirpes* and equally between them their deceased parent's share. A child conceived prior to but born during its parents' marriage is legitimate. Children adopted by the full adoption procedure have all the rights of a legitimate child; those adopted under the 'simple' procedure have inheritance rights only in the estates of their adopting parents but without losing their rights in respect of their original family. Hence children adopted by the 'simple' procedure cannot take by representation any share which a predeceased adopting parent would have taken in the intestacies of that parent's parents or brothers or sisters. 'Adulterine' children count as illegitimate children but their share in an intestate estate may be diminished in certain circumstances (see Chapter 18).

Articles 746 et seq of the Code Civil provide as follows:

1. If there are no surviving children or issue of the intestate *and no surviving mother or father*, brothers and sisters share *per capita*, their issue taking *per stirpes* by representation their deceased parent's share in the estate. If the brothers or sisters are not all children of the same marriage as the intestate, a special method of distribution applies.

2. If there are no surviving children or issue of the intestate *but a surviving mother and/or father*, each of such parents takes a quarter of the estate absolutely, the remaining half or three-quarters being divisible as in 1. above.

3. In default of surviving children or issue, brothers or sisters or their issue or mother and father, ascendants more distant than mother and father are entitled to share in the estate. The estate is divided into two parts, one for the paternal and one for the maternal line. The ascendants nearest in degree to the intestate in each line takes that half share, taking *per capita* if more than one. If there are no ascendants in one line (subject to 4 below), the whole estate passes to the ascendants in the other line.

4. A surviving spouse is entitled as follows:

(i) If there are no surviving children or issue or brothers or sisters or their issue *and no ascendants*, the surviving spouse takes the whole of the estate absolutely.

(ii) If there are surviving ascendants in one line only, the surviving spouse takes the share of the other line, i.e. one quarter of the estate.

(iii) If a surviving spouse takes no absolute interest in either of the cases referred to above, he or she is entitled to a life interest in either (a) a quarter of the estate if the deceased left one or more legitimate or illegitimate (but not 'adulterine') children or (b) a half of the estate if the deceased left 'adulterine' children only or brothers or sisters or their issue or ascendants more remote than in the first degree.

22   Stamp Duties and Death Duties

Stamp Duties

The heading to this chapter correctly combines two different kinds of fiscal impositions, since both are *droits d'enregistrement*, but it must be admitted that 'Stamp Duties' is not a wholly correct translation of those *droits d'enregistrement* which are referred to in this book by that phrase. In fact, *droits de timbre*, which can faithfully be translated as 'Stamp Duties' also exist in France. Perhaps the most well known is the *vignette*, the Road Fund Tax. Others include stamps on entrance cards to casinos, certain documents for the transport of freight, French nationals' identity cards and foreigners' *cartes de séjour* and some Stock Exchange documents. *Papier timbré* that is to say, sheets of paper with Revenue stamps already printed on them can still be bought and used for documents which require a stamp of the value available in this way. One can also buy (though often this involves considerable searching) adhesive *timbres fiscaux*. One still sees in references to documents required for certain administrative purposes the phrase '*sur papier libre*', i.e. the transaction recorded bears no stamp duty.

There are many fixed and *ad valorem droits d'enregistrement*. In so far as this type of duty is concerned, this chapter treats only those which are connected with the purchase of land. These, when *ad valorem*, are payable to the *Département* in which the property is situate and are known as *droit départemental d'enregistrement*. To this must be added a *taxe locale* and a *taxe régionale*. A final addition is made based on the *droit départemental* found due, which is to cover the State for the cost of collecting tax for the benefit of the *Départements*. The basic rate is variable by the annual Loi des Finances; the *taxe régionale* is fixed annually by each region and, with few exceptions, tends to be the same all over France.

The various rates of Stamp Duty appear in Appendix B. For the reader who prefers first to complete reading of this chapter, let it be said that, if the full *ad valorem* rate were chargeable on a transaction in which he was involved, it would be not far short of twenty per cent, but let him take much-needed comfort from the thought that it is extremely unlikely that he will have been involved in a transaction bearing that exorbitant rate. Even so, the rate on many an ordinary house purchase is high.

The most usual circumstances in which reduced *ad valorem* rates are chargeable are described below. Where such conditions as must be fulfilled to obtain a reduced rate are not complied with, payment of the balance of the full duty becomes exigible plus a penalty, sometimes in the form of extra duty and sometimes in the form of interest, which may in certain circumstances in part or in whole be remitted.

1. (i) Buildings or parts of buildings and their appurtenances, whether these are bought at the same time as the main property or separately for use as private dwelling-houses, qualify for a reduced rate. In such cases, in about two-thirds of the *Départements*, the joint *départemental* and local rate is reduced by a standard amount to about a quarter of the full rate. The remaining *Départements* also allow considerable reductions, in some cases a little more and in some cases a little less than the standard amount.

(ii) Land on which is built property which would qualify for the reduced rate as in (i) above to the extent of 2,500 square metres. Land over that area (it may sometimes be increased to 5,000 square metres) must be separately valued and stamped at a higher rate.

(iii) In order to obtain this reduced rate, the purchaser must undertake in the *acte de vente* to use the premises as a dwelling-house only for a period of three years.

(iv) Demolition of a property, in respect of which such an undertaking has been given, with a view to rebuilding, in principle gives rise to the subsequent payment of full duty plus penalty but in certain circumstances this will not be charged and the purchaser will be allowed to opt for the *régime de la TVA immobilière* (see below).

(v) The reduced rates do not apply to tax-haven company

purchasers (see Chapter 10).

2. Building-land or houses or flats which are subject to the TVA regime are liable only to a very reduced rate of duty. This affects many new flats and houses and explains the phrase '*frais de notaire réduits*'. The circumstances in which this reduced rate is available are explained below.

3. A small reduction in rate is available for buildings 'of a rural nature'. The test is not the situation of the building but its character, so that one can enjoy this reduction (if no better reduction is available) on a *rus in urbe* principle, and a 'rural' building can qualify even if it is in the centre of a town.

4. Certain buildings bought with a view to the increase of the profits of a farm or similar agricultural business, provided that a certain minimum area results, enjoy a reduced rate of *droit départemental*.

5. Subject to certain conditions, part of the purchase price of agricultural property bought by young agriculturalists (aged between twenty-one and thirty-five) who can prove their farming ability is charged at a reduced rate.

6. A very significant reduction in rate is given to farmers on the purchase of agricultural property where, immediately prior to purchase, it was held on lease continuously for an agricultural user by them or their ascendants or their spouses or their spouses' ascendants and lodged with the *enregistrement* or disclosed to the tax authorities, which will usually result from the annual payment of *droit de bail*, at least two years before the date of purchase. A purchaser must undertake for himself and his successors in title as to the future working of the land. The reduction applies also where the lease in question has come into the ownership of the purchaser or any of the other persons mentioned above by assignment provided that that assignment took place two years before completion of the purchase.

7. The purchase of woodlands, land acquired for business purposes with a view to the reduction of unemployment or for scientific research, training centres or agricultural co-operatives, among other land with special users, is also subject to a reduced rate of stamp duty.

Most building land is subject to TVA. In such circumstances, no stamp duties are payable but the purchaser pays the tax on the sale price at the standard rate. Certain buildings are also subject on sale to the payment of TVA and in these circumstances no duty is payable. The sale price of buildings or parts of buildings (i.e. flats) sold prior to completion of the building works are subject to TVA. This will be paid by the seller and the *acte de vente* will show the price divided between the sale price itself and the TVA payable on it.

On a sale of a building or the part of a building within five years of its completion, TVA is payable on the sale price by the seller and again no stamp duty is payable. This concession applies only to the first sale after the completion of the building unless the intermediate sale was to a *marchand de biens*. Such a person is defined as one whose business is the purchase of assets (in this case, property) with a view to their resale at a profit. On the whole, first sales within this first five-year period are normally purchases from private individuals. It does happen that persons buy up a few flats in a block at a global and therefore reduced price with a view to resale at a profit, but they are frequently small private investors and are not treated as *marchands de biens*. It must be remembered that on such a sale the benefit accrues to the buyer. The seller is liable to TVA on the difference between his purchase price ex-TVA and his sale price. In practice, unless the rate of TVA changes noticeably, a resale within a five-year period will not attract such an increase in value as to make this liability very onerous.

The stamp duty on mortgages which appears in Appendix B is chargeable whether the mortgage is contemporaneous with a purchase or not. The duty on a release is a fixed duty.

Powers of Attorney executed in France in the form of an *acte notarié* are subject to a fixed duty; those executed *s.s.p.*, unless voluntarily presented for stamping, are free of duty. A Power executed out of France for use in France does not require stamping in France.

Death Duties

Save to the extent that there may from time to time be in force reductions in respect of gifts *inter vivos*, the duty payable on a death and on a gift *inter vivos* is the same and the duties are treated under one head in France.

In cases where the deceased left no assets or where the gross assets do not exceed 10,000 francs and the beneficiaries are either children and issue or surviving spouse, no *déclaration de succession*, which is the equivalent of an Inheritance Tax Account, need be filed. In the case of a person domiciled in France, subject to the provisions of any tax treaty, all his assets both real and personal wherever they may be situate must be disclosed. In the case of persons not domiciled in France, only assets situate or deemed to be situate in France need to be disclosed.

Domicile in France for the purpose of the payment of death duties means fiscal domicile. In practice this differs little from residence for tax purposes in the UK but officially it is acquired if a person (i) himself or through his immediate family, i.e. wife and children has his home (*foyer*) in France or (ii) is a regular visitor to France, the criterion being to spend 183 days or more in France in any one year or (iii) carries on a 'professional activity' in France, unless it is ancillary to activities carried on elsewhere, or (iv) uses France as the centre of his economic interests, i.e. has most of his investments in or obtains the major part of his income from or manages generally his affairs from France.

It is, of course, necessary to have regard to the effect of Double Tax Conventions as to the situs of assets, but this matter is not dealt with in this book. It must, however, be noted that the ownership of shares in non-French companies whose assets consist primarily (that is to say, according to the French Revenue, in excess of fifty per cent of their total assets) of realty in France gives rise to a liability to duty on death of a shareholder unless the company in question is one which has paid its annual three per cent tax (see Chapter 10).

The *déclaration de succession* states the terms of the deceased's Will (if any), full details of the beneficiaries in the estate and details of all gifts made *inter vivos* by the deceased. It should be signed by all the beneficiaries or Attorneys on their behalf and this need present no difficulty. It should be filed within six months of the date of death if the deceased died in France or one year if he died elsewhere, after which interest begins to run. It is filed at the tax office of the district where the deceased habitually resided or, if he died domiciled out of France, with the office in Paris which deals with non-residents' tax affairs.

As with an Inheritance Tax Account, all assets must be listed, whether they are exempt or not, and an estimated or actual value given. Personal chattels, unless their value is supported by a detailed professional valuation and subject to proof to the contrary, are deemed to be of a value equal to five per cent of the total of all other assets of the deceased. It is to be noted the insurance companies are required by law to inform the tax authorities on a death of all insurances they have written on jewellery, *objets d'art* and the like belonging to the deceased. In addition, every insurance company is required to report annually to the tax authorities every policy it writes in respect of similar assets in amounts exceeding 100,000 francs. As to liabilities which may be deducted, in principle, all debts in existence at the date of death are allowable (with the exception of those whose acceptance it is said would lead to tax evasion), as are medical fees for the deceased's last illness without limit, and funeral expenses up to 3,000 francs an amount which at the date of this book represents about one third of the poorest funeral available in France. Such a deduction is allowed on proof of its payment but with unexpected generosity, if the amount is 1,000 francs or less, no proof of expenditure is required.

Certain assets are exempt from duty. Life policies effected for the benefit of named beneficiaries or their heirs do not, if certain conditions are fulfilled, form part of a deceased's estate. In the case of such policies, the deceased must have been aged at least sixty-six when the policy was written and the total of the first four years' premium or (if such is the case) the single premium payable must represent at least three-quarters of the sum assured. Provision is made for the situation where more than one policy has been effected. Beneficiaries are required to notify the Revenue of such policies but the assurers themselves may not pay out the policy moneys unless presented with a certificate of duty paid or of exemption from duty or at a beneficiary's request to use the moneys for the payment direct of duty on some asset which is dutiable.

Other exempt assets include reversions to *viager* rents between spouses and ascendants in the direct line, a proportion of the value of woodlands and of long leases of rural properties and works of art and collections of historic or artistic value which are bequeathed to the State or a municipality.

The table for valuing life interest and reversions is to be found in Appendix B.

A special exception exists in respect of realty (but not personalty) owned *en tontine*. If the property is at the death of a co-owner worth not more than 500,000 francs and if it is then occupied as the principal private of both co-owners, *droits de succession* are not charged but stamp duty at approximately 8% only is charged.

In the case of bequests to the State and, in very general terms, to charities, no duty is payable, but English criteria do not run in France, and it is wise to make enquiries, except in the most obvious cases, when making gifts of this nature to establish whether they are duty-free or subject to duty at sixty per cent.

Duty, at least as calculated for each beneficiary by the person preparing the account, is payable on filing the *déclaration de succession*. Duties may be paid by instalments and payment may in certain circumstances be deferred. The basic period over which payment by instalments may be made is five years but this may be extended to ten years in the case of beneficiaries who are surviving spouses or in the direct line and if certain types of non-liquid assets comprise the bequest in question. Interest is chargeable at the rate applicable to certain types of gilt-edged securities at the day when application for payment by instalments is made and remains fixed throughout the instalment period. Payment by instalments must be supported by suitable security, which can be in the nature of a charge on the property which gives rise to the duty liability or on other real or personal property and must be in double the amount of the unpaid duty.

Payment of duty may be deferred in the case of bequests of reversions until six months after they fall in. Interest need not be paid if the duty ultimately payable is calculated not on the value of the reversion but on the value of the property free of the life interest as at the date of death of the deceased. Payment of duty may also be deferred when a gift *inter vivos* has been made to a beneficiary who is not a *héritier réservataire* which has eaten into the *réserve* (see Chapter

18). Duty in respect of the amount to be repaid to the *héritier réservataire* may be deferred until distribution takes place.

In circumstances in which it is available, relief from UK Inheritance Tax in respect of *droits de succession* paid in France may be obtained under the current Double Tax Convention. The necessary form should be obtained from Minford House and after completion returned there for it to be forwarded to France for certification. It is not possible to give any indication of how long that process may take. It must also be remembered that there is no surviving spouse exemption in France.

The rates of Stamp Duties and Death Duties current at the date of publication of this book are set out in Appendix B. Rates rarely vary during a calendar year, variations being effected by the annual *Loi des Finances* which is passed towards the end of every year and takes effect on 1 January next ensuing.

Appendix A: Precedents

The following precedents have been included primarily as a matter of interest and their inclusion should not be taken as an indication that they can safely be used without the guidance of someone familiar with French procedure.

No precedents for an *acte de vente* or for leases have been included, since such documents are unlikely to be prepared out of France, nor can proper advice on them, except from a very limited number of advisers, be obtained in England. French Wills cannot, of course, safely be prepared except by those conversant with French law but as a matter of interest a single precedent is included. The main choice has fallen on documents in which advisers in England are most likely actively to be involved, the intention being that the comments as well as the precedents themselves may be of assistance in understanding some of the processes referred to in this book. The series '*Ce qu'il vous faut savoir*' (J. Delmas et Cie, Paris) contains a vast variety of precedents and explanations. Care must, however, be taken that the book in the series referred to is up to date and it must be remembered that they are intended for the intelligent layman and not for the lawyer.

Most of the precedents appearing below are in French and translations are usually not provided for the reasons given in the Introduction. Points of importance are, however, explained. In one or two cases, the precedent is in English only. These are documents which could emanate from the U.K. and be used in that form in France accompanied by a French translation.

In this connection, it is necessary to add a word on translations generally. Strictly speaking, every translation into French for official use, i.e. by a Notary, a Court or a local Companies Registry, should be made by a *traducteur juré*. Luckily, in many cases, Notaries will accept translations by someone whom they know is capable of producing a correct result, provided the translation is certified as a faithful translation and the translator is a member of a suitable profession, e.g. a Solicitor or Member of the Bar. But if formal translations are needed (very often this depends on the decision of a Civil Servant) it is worth remembering that the cost of translations by *traducteurs jurés* is very high and that they are not always wholly accurate in the case of legal documents. In certain cases it can be well worthwhile approaching a suitable Notary Public in the U.K. whose translations are acceptable in France and accurate.

The following precedent is one of those prepared by FNAIM, 129, rue du Faubourg-Saint-Honoré, 75008 Paris. It is used by many of the leading Estate Agents in France and whilst the use of other forms, particularly if they are prepared by Notaries or other lawyers may differ substantially, the use of any form of contract prepared by FNAIM is a guarantee of its basic suitability. This does not, however, detract from the significance of the advice that generally speaking any contract for the purchase or sale of real property handed out by an Estate Agent in France for signature should not be signed until it has been approved by some suitably qualified person or that in certain circumstances, alterations or additions to the draft may not be desirable. The precedent chosen is that for the purchase of a flat in a block because the majority of English purchasers buy flats. For obvious reasons, if the property involved is a house or building land, the need for suitable advice is that much more significant.

The precedent as printed makes no obvious reference to the Loi Scrivener condition. Two standard clauses – one for where no loan is being obtained and one where mortgage finance is being sought – have been added in French and English at the end of the precedent.

Care must be taken with the clause dealing with the seller's Agent's commission. It is frequent for an Estate Agent to quote to his seller client a 'net' price, that is to say a sale price less commission. He will then endeavour to obtain from a purchaser a 'gross' price which will be the amount shown in the clause which deals with the price and on which will be based the notarial fees, Stamp Duties etc. The commission clause should therefore show that the commission is the liability of the seller. On occasions, the sale price will be the 'net' price and the buyer will pay the commission. In such circumstances, it is on the net price plus the commission that fees and Stamp Duties are calculated. In certain parts of France special local rules apply to the payment of commission. Care must also be taken when certain types of contracts are handed out that the liability to commission is not shown as that of purchaser and vendor jointly and severally.

In French conveyances, the sale price cannot be expressed solely in foreign currency. If what is involved is a sale between two non-French parties, there is no reason why in the contract the price should not be shown in a non-French currency but it should therefore contain a provision for the ascertainment of the proper rate of exchange, preferably at the date of contract or of completion, in Paris or in London, buying, selling or mid-rate etc. so that the draft *acte de vente* submitted for CGT purposes contains the correct franc price.

The use of technical phrases in the translation which follows the original French must not be taken as implying that these phrases have the same meaning in French law as they have in English law.

COMPROMIS POUR VENTE D'APPARTEMENT EN COPROPRIÉTÉ

Entre les soussignés:

M [*vendor*]   d'une part;

Et M [*Purchaser*]   d'autre part;

Il est convenu et réciproquement arrêté ce qui suit:

M [*vendor*] vend par les présentes en s'obligeant à toutes les garanties ordinaires de fait et de droit en pareilles matières, les parties ci-après désignées de l'immeuble dénommé [*name of building*] situé à [*address*]

DÉSIGNATION

Parties divises. – Un appartement situé au [*floor number*] étage, formant le lot [*lot number*] du cahier des charges et se composant de [*description*]:

Parties indivises. – Et la copropriété de toutes choses communes en général dudit immeuble et de ses dépendances, telles qu'elles sont déterminées et réparties dans le cahier des charges, et le règlement de copropriété dont l'acquéreur déclare avoir eu complète connaissance.

ORIGINE DE PROPRIÉTÉ

Il sera établi un acte de propriété, comportant les origines de propriété régulières des parties qui font l'objet de la présente vente et il y sera fait par le vendeur toutes déclarations d'état civil et autres d'usage. Les parties dispensent le rédacteur des présentes d'en établir de plus amples.

ENTRÉE EN JOUISSANCE

L'acquéreur sera propriétaire desdites parties d'immeuble par le fait des présentes et leur réitération par acte authentique. Il en aura jouissance par [*event giving possession*]

L'acquéreur prendra lesdites parties d'immeuble dans leur état actuel, déclarant bien les connaître pour les avoir visitées.

Il acquittera, à compter du jour de son entrée en jouissance, les contributions et charges de toutes natures et notamment les charges de copropriété qui seront dues et qui pourront grever les parties d'immeuble acquises par lui.

PRIX

La présente vente est faite et réciproquement acceptée moyennant le prix principal de [*price*] francs sur lequel l'acquéreur a versé à l'instant même au vendeur qui le reconnaît et lui en donne bonne et valable quittance, la somme de F:

DONT QUITTANCE

Le solde, soit la somme de [*balance of price*]
sera payable comme suit:

[*See below for Loi Scrivener declarations*]

SERVITUDES ET CONDITIONS PARTICULIÈRES

L'acquéreur jouira des servitudes actives et souffrira celles passives. A cet égard, le vendeur déclare que personnellement il n'a creé ni laissé acquérir aucune servitude sur l'immeuble dont il s'agit et qu'à sa connaissance il n'en existe pas d'autres et celles pouvant résulter des titres de propriété, du cahier des charges, du règlement de copropriété, de la loi des règlements municipaux et de tous plans d'aménagements, d'extension ou d'embellissement de la ville.

L'acquéreur sera tenu à l'exécution pleine et entière de toutes clauses concernant les charges, clauses, conditions et servitudes du règlement de copropriété dudit immeuble.

RÉITÉRATION

Les présentes seront, de convention expresse, réitérées par acte authentique par-devant Maître [*name of notary*], notaire à [*address of notary*], choisi d'un commun accord entre les parties, au plus tard. [*date of completion*]

L'acquéreur prendra à sa charge tous les frais, droits et le honoraires de la vente et de ses suites.

Le privilège et l'action résolutoire seront expressément réservés par le vendeur à la garantie du paiement du prix dans les termes et conditions qui viennent d'être stipulés.

M [*vendor*] ès qualité déclare que l'immeuble vendu n'est grevé d'aucune hypothéque ni d'aucune servitude autre que celles résultant du cahier des charges, du règlement de copropriété et de l'acte d'acquisition, ou s'il s'en révélait à la transcription, le vendeur s'oblige d'en donner la mainlevée dans le mois qui suivrait la dénonciation qui lui en serait faite par simple lettre recommandée.

RÉMUNÉRATION DE L'AGENT IMMOBILIER

Les parties reconnaissent avoir été mises en contact et être parvenues à un accord, par les soins de Monsieur [*name of agent*] Agent immobilier, demeurant à [*address of agent*]

Pour son intervention, Monsieur [*agent*] percevra une commission de   Francs taxes comprises.

Cette rémunération sera à la charge du [*vendor/purchaser*] et sera exigible à compter de ce jour du fait même de la signature des présentes qui ne comportent aucune condition suspensive.

ÉLECTION DE DOMICILE

Pour l'exécution des présentes et de l'acte authentique à intervenir, les parties font élection de domicile à: [*address for service*]

Fait de bonne foi, à [*place*], le [*date*]

En autant d'exemplaires que de parties.

LOI SCRIVENER DECLARATIONS

If the Purchaser is buying without the aid of a loan, the following clause (the wording but not the clear intent of which may slightly vary in each case) should be included:
'Je déclare effectuer cette acquisition sans recourir à aucun prêt. Je reconnais avoir été informé que si je recours néanmoins à un pret, je ne pourrai me prévaloir de la condition suspensive de son obtention prévue par la Loi N° 79-596 du 13 juillet 1979.'

If the Purchaser intends obtaining mortgage finance for his purchase, the form of declaration could be substantially as follows:
'En application des Articles 16 et 17 de la Loi du 13 juillet 1979, je précise que le prix de vente sera payé à l'aide du pret que je me propose de contracter à [*name and address of Lender*]. Ce prêt sera consenti par cet établissement aux conditions et selon les modalités habituelles dont je déclare avoir déjà pris connaissance et pour lequel l'intéret et les annuités de remboursement m'ont déjà été précisés par l'établissement susnommé.'

In each case, the declaration must be in the handwriting of the Purchaser and it is usual to ask for a signature to the clause in addition to the signature at the end of the contract. The translations of the above declarations are as follows:

(Where no loan is being sought)
'I declare that I make this purchase without recourse to any loan. I confirm that I have been informed that if nevertheless hereafter I seek a loan I am not entitled to the protection afforded by the condition precedent referring to the obtaining of such a loan provided for in Law N° 79-596 of 13 July 1979.'

(Where a loan is being sought)
'Pursuant to Clauses 16 and 17 of the Law No. 79-596 of 13 July 1979 I confirm that the purchase price will be found in part by a loan which I intend obtaining from (name and address of Lender). This loan will be granted by that Institution upon usual terms of which I declare already to have knowledge and at a rate of interest and with provisions for repayment which have already been communicated to me.'

CONTRACT FOR THE SALE OF A CONDOMINIUM FLAT

BETWEEN

(Name and address of Vendor)

of the one part

and　　　　　　(Name and address of Purchaser)

of the other part

WHEREBY IT IS AGREED AS FOLLOWS:

Mr [*Vendor*] by virtue of these presents sells with the benefit of the warranties implied in fact and by law[1] those parts hereinafter described of the building known as and situate at [*description of property sold*]

DESCRIPTION

Private Parts of the Building[2] – A flat situated on the [–th] floor being Lot number   in the cahier des charges and consisting of [*description of flat – usually including number of rooms and area of flat and balcony (if any) and cellar and garage or parking space (if any) which each will have a Lot number*]

Common Parts of the Building[2] – And the undivided share in the common parts of the said building and its appurtenances as the same is described and quantified in the cahier des charges and the règlement de copropriété the contents of both of which the Purchaser declares that he has full knowledge.

TITLE

The conveyance hereafter to be executed shall include the deduction of the title of the Vendor to the property hereby agreed to be sold and all declarations as to his état civil and other matters usually made And the parties hereto dispense the draftsman hereof from further reference herein to such matters.

POSSESSION

The property in the said parts of the said building shall become vested in the Purchaser by virtue of these presents and the execution of the acte authentique pursuant hereto and he shall have possession on [*date on which possession will be given*]. The Purchaser having inspected the same shall take the property in the state in which it is at the date hereof. The Purchaser shall as from the date on which he takes possession discharge all outgoings in respect of the property and in particular the Service Charges affecting the same as and when they may become due.

SALE PRICE

The said property is sold and purchased at the price of [*sale price*] of which the Purchaser has on the execution hereof paid the sum of [*deposit*] the receipt of which the Vendor hereby acknowledges. The balance of the said price shall be payable [*details of payment at completion, i.e. all by the Purchaser or part by the Purchaser and part by a Mortgagee etc.*] (Insert here in the handwriting of the Purchaser the Loi Scrivener clause.[3])

EASEMENTS AND SPECIAL CONDITIONS

The property is sold subject to and with the benefit of such easements and rights affecting the same as may exist at the date hereof. The Vendor declares that he has not himself granted or suffered the grant of any easement or right over the property and that no easements or rights exist other than those disclosed by the title of the Vendor the cahier des charges or the règlement de copropriété or arising by reason of any municipal regulation or development extension or improvement scheme. The Purchaser will in all respects abide by the various provisions of the règlement de copropriété of the said building

COMPLETION

It is agreed that the intent of these presents shall be comprised in an acte authentique executed before Maître of [*name and address of Notary*][4] instructed by agreement by both the parties hereto not later than the [*date of completion*]. All costs duties and other expenses of this sale shall be borne by the Purchaser.[5]

The Vendor declares that the property sold is free of all encumbrances and easements other than those disclosed in the cahier des charges the règlement de copropriété or the conveyance to the Vendor. In the event of a Land Registry search revealing any other encumbrance or easement the Vendor will within one month of notice to that effect being served on him by registered letter post obtain a release therefrom.

ESTATE AGENT'S COMMISSION

The parties hereto agree that they were placed in communication one with the other and entered into this Agreement through the good offices of [*name and address of Estate Agent*] for which he shall be entitled to commission of francs inclusive of VAT. [*The Purchaser/The Vendor*] is liable for the payment of this commission which is due and payable by reason of the execution of this Agreement which is unconditional.[6]

ADDRESS FOR SERVICE

In connection with the execution of this Agreement and of the acte authentique hereafter to be executed the parties respective addresses for service are:

Signed this – day of – 19– in as many copies as there are parties.

Notes

1. There is no equivalent in English law of the French '*les garanties ordinaires de fait et de droit*', which appears in many documents covering many transactions. Its implication is evident and in the case of a conveyancing document 'as beneficial owner' at least imparts some of the flavour of the obligations comprised in the phrase.

2. What is owned *en copropriété* i.e. the common parts of the building owned in undivided shares; unfortunately, the opposite of an undivided share is more difficult to translate and it is neither freehold nor leasehold. See chapter 11.

3. The Loi Scrivener clause will be in the form appropriate to the circumstances as shown on pp. 168–9. It must be emphasized that they can vary considerably in content. If a purchaser who has said in the contract that he is obtaining mortgage finance decides not to do so it is desirable to obtain his confirmation in writing and warn him of the effect.

4. Even if but one Notary is shown here, each party may subsequently instruct his own Notary. Most contracts when handed out will show the Notary chosen by the Seller. Since the Purchaser has choice of Notary, if the Seller wishes to retain the services of his Notary, it is desirable that the contract indicate this. One would then add the name of the Buyer's Notary as 'assisting' or 'collaborating'. See Chapter 3.

5. This precedent does not contain any special provisions for default on the part of one or the other party. Most contracts will, in fact, contain a clause to cover one or other of the methods referred to in Chapter 3 to deal with such defaults.

6. Many contracts will not be unconditional at the time of execution.

Powers of Attorney

PURCHASES AND SALE OF PROPERTY

The Union International du Notariat Latin provides precedents for a variety of Powers of Attorney and that for a purchase of property appears below. It should presumably, in the light of its origin, always be acceptable in France but there are certain minor aspects of which some Notaries have evinced dislike and an alternative in slightly different form is therefore included.

There is a school of thought which holds that, since the Loi Scrivener declaration in both the *compromis de vente* and the *acte de vente* should be in the handwriting of the buyer, a Power of Attorney to buy land should give the donee special power to do this include the declaration in the handwriting of the donor. See Chapter 6 as to this declaration. It would seem that most Notaries in France do not subscribe to this view and that a general power to make declarations required by law not in the handwriting of the donor will suffice.

The form suggested by the Union Internationale authorizes the Attorney 'to buy at such price and subject to such conditions as the Attorney considers fit'. The alternative form gives a similar power but in respect of an expressed price. Which to use is a matter for the donor of the Power but, whilst most Notaries will accept a Power with a price expressed which is greater than the actual purchase price (or, in the case of a sale, if the sale price exceeds that at which the Attorney is authorized to sell), by no means all will do this. Most Powers will be given after a contract has been executed and in those circumstances it seems wise to show the known sale or purchase price.

Nor does the Union Internationale form hint that the price can be paid *hors vue de notaire*, and many Notaries will not agree to complete with Attorneys present unless they are covered by a reference to this means of payment in the Power of Attorney. Finally, it makes no reference to *tontine* purchases the inclusion of which is a serious safeguard for donors intending so to buy.

The alternative form which experiences has shown to be preferable includes the power for the Attorney to deal with loans, which can, of course, be omitted if it will not be used. There is no such power in the Union Internationale Power.

In the alternative form appropriate wording for purchases by joint owners is shown which is not catered for in the shorter form.

UNION INTERNATIONALE DU NOTARIAT LATIN POWER OF ATTORNEY TO BUY PROPERTY

PROCURATION
L'AN MIL NEUF CENT QUATRE VINGT –
Et le –
PARDEVANT –

A COMPARU

Monsieur [*surname*], [*first names*], [*occupation*], né le [*date of birth*] à [*place of birth*] et Madame [*maiden surname*], [*first names*] son épouse, [*occupation*], née le [*date of birth*] à [*place of birth*], demeurant ensemble à [*place of residence*], de nationalité britannique, mariés sous le régime anglais équivalent au régime français de la séparation de biens à défaut de contrat de mariage préalable à leur union célébrée le [*date of marriage*] à [*place of marriage*]

Ci-après denommé 'Le Mandant'

Le Mandant a par les présentes déclaré constituer pour mandataire spécial

Monsieur [*name, occupation and address of attorney*]

A qui il donne pouvoir pour lui et en son nom:

Acquérir aux prix charges et conditions que le mandataire jugera convenables

[*Description of property to be bought as in following precedent*]

PAYER le prix comptant ou obliger le mandant à son paiement en principal et intérêts aux époques et de la manière qui seront stipulées ainsi qu'à l'exécution des charges et conditions qui seront imposées

FAIRE toutes déclarations et affirmations prescrites par la loi

EXIGER toutes justifications, se faire remettre tous titres et pièces en donnant décharge

SIGNER tous contrats de vente ou procès-verbaux d'adjudication

FAIRE procéder à toutes formalités aux livres ou registres fonciers

FAIRE toutes dénonciations notifications et offres de paiement, provoquer tous ordres

PAYER le prix d'acquisition entre les mains des vendeurs ou des créanciers inscrits faire toutes consignations

AUX effets ci-dessus passer et signer tous actes et pièces, élire domicile, faire toutes déclarations d'état civil et généralement faire tout ce qui sera necessaire ou utile même non explicitement prévu aux présentes

DONT ACTE en brevet

Etabli en – pages

FAIT ET PASSE A –

ALTERNATIVE FORM OF POWER OF ATTORNEY TO BUY PROPERTY

PROCURATION

L'AN MIL NEUF CENT QUATRE VINGT –

Et le –

PARDEVANT –

A COMPARU

Monsieur [*surname*], [*first names*], [*occupation*], né le [*date of birth*] à [*place of birth*] et Madame [*maiden surname*], [*first names*] son épouse, [*occupation*], née le [*date of birth*] à [*place of birth*], demeurant ensemble à [*place of residence*], de nationalité britannique, mariés sous le régime anglais équivalent au régime français de la séparation de biens à défaut de contrat de mariage préalable à leur union célébrée le [*date of marriage*] à [*place of marriage*]

Ci-après denommé 'Le Constituant'

LEQUEL a par ces présents constitué pour son mandataire

Monsieur [*name, occupation and address of attorney*]

A QUI il donne pouvoir pour lui et en son nom:

ACQUERIR sous les charges et conditions que le mandataire jugera convenables moyennant le prix de (*price in figures*) francs (*price in words*) FRANCS (payable hors vue de notaire) (en indivision à concurrence de (*proportions in which the undivided shares are owned*)) (en tontine le (surplus du) prix étant assuré à concurrence de la moitié des deniers personnels de chacun des constituants les biens et droits ci-après (*cadastral description of the property*) savoir:

LOT NUMERO [number of lot]

UN APPARTEMENT [*short description of flat etc*] avec les [*proportion*] des parties spéciales du bâtiment et [*proportion*] des parties communes générales

(EMPRUNTER jusqu'à la somme principale de [*maximum amount of loan*] francs des personnes, au taux, pour le temps et sous les conditions que le mandataire avisera et obliger le constituant au remboursement du capital et au service des intérêts aux époques et de la manière qui seront convenus)

OBLIGER le constituant au paiement du solde du prix aux époques et de la manière qui seront convenus ainsi qu'à l'exécution des charges qui seront imposées, se faire remettre tous titres et pièces, en donner décharge

FAIRE opérer conformément à la législation en vigueur tous transferts et mouvements de fonds

FAIRE toutes affirmations prescrites par la loi relativement à la sincérité du prix

(*If the Donor is not obtaining a loan*) APPOSER la mention prescrite par l'article 18 de la loi du 13 juillet 1979 que le constituant n'envisage pas de contracter aucun emprunt (*or if the Donor is obtaining a loan*) APPOSER la mention prescrite par l'article 18 de la loi du 13 juillet 1979 et déclarer que pour le financement de l'acquisition ci-dessus, le Constituant n'envisage pas de contracter d'autre emprunt que celui dont il est question ci-dessus

FAIRE opérer toutes publicités foncières purges dénonciations notifications et offres de paiement provoquer faire toutes demandes en mainlevée et exercer toutes actions pour l'exécution du contrat

FAIRE toutes déclarations d'états civil et autres

AUX effets ci-dessus passer et signer tous actes et pièces élire domicile substituer et généralement faire tout ce qui sera utile ou nécessaire

DONT ACTE en brevet
Etabli en – pages
FAIT ET PASSE A –

POWER OF ATTORNEY TO SELL PROPERTY

PROCURATION
L'AN MIL NEUF CENT QUATRE VINGT–

et le –
PARDEVANT –

A COMPARU

Monsieur [*état civil as in previous power of attorney*]
Ci-après denommé 'Le Constituant'
LEQUEL a par ces présentes constitué pour son mandataire
[*name, occupation and address of attorney*]
A QUI il donne pouvoir pour lui et en son nom:
VENDRE sous les charges et conditions que le mandataire
jugera convenables moyennant le prix de [*price in figures*] francs
[*price in words*] francs (payable hors vue de notaire) les biens et
droits ci-après [*cadastral description of the property*] savoir:
LOT NUMERO [*number of lot*]
UN APPARTEMENT [*short description of flat etc*] avec les
[*proportion*] des parties spéciales du bâtiment et [*proportion*]
des parties communes générales
ETABLIR la désignation complète et l'origine de propriété
dudit immeuble, faire dresser tout cahier de charge, faire toutes
déclarations relatives aux locations, stipuler toutes servitudes
OBLIGER le comparant à toutes garanties et au rapport de
toutes mainlevées et certificats de radiations, ainsi que de toutes
justifications qu'il y aura lieu, fixer l'époque d'entrée en
jouissance, convenir du mode et des époques de paiement du
prix, le recevoir en principal et intérêts, soit comptant soit aux
termes convenus ou par anticipation
FAIRE toutes déclarations d'état civil et autres et toutes
affirmations prescrites par la loi relativement à la sincerité du
prix qui sera stipulé
SIGNER toute déclaration de plus-value, désigner un
représantant fiscal accredité, payer toutes taxes imposées sur la
plus-value, signer toute demande de dispense de la désignation
d'un représantant fiscal accredité
A défaut de paiement et en cas de difficultés quelconques,
exercer toutes les poursuites nécessaires depuis la conciliation
jusqu'à l'entière exécution de tous jugements et arrêts par les
voies et moyens de droit, en tout état de cause, traiter, transiger
et compromettre, produire à tous ordres et distribution, toucher
le montant de toutes collocations au profit du comparant
DE toutes sommes reçues donner quittances et décharges,
consentir mentions et subrogations, avec ou sans garantie,
donner mainlevée avec désistement de tous droits de privilège,
hypothèque et action résolutoire, consentir à la radiation de
toutes inscriptions de privilège de vendeur ou autres, le tout avec

2ou sans constation de paiement, remettre tous titres et pièces ou obliger le constituant à leur remise

AUX effets ci-dessus, passer et signer tous actes, élire domicile, substituer et généralement faire le nécessaire.

DONT ACTE EN BREVET

Etabli en – pages

FAIT ET PASSE A –

POWER OF ATTORNEY TO ADMINISTER AN ESTATE

The following Power contains all that will normally be necessary to deal with the estate of a person domiciled (or not) in France in respect of French assets. If there are unusual assets or circumstances involved, it may be desirable to widen further the powers given to the Attorney. Normally each residuary beneficiary appointed by a Will or beneficiary entitled under entrenched rights of inheritance or entitled on an intestacy who does not want to deal personally will have to appoint an Attorney. Whether all make one Power and appoint one Attorney or there are several Powers and one or more Attorneys must depend on circumstances. The following precedent assumes a single beneficiary donor.

PROCURATION

L'AN MIL NEUF CENT QUATRE VINGT–

Et le –

PARDEVANT –

A COMPARU

Monsieur [*full details of donor's* état civil *as in previous precedents*]

Ci-après dénommé 'Le Constituant'

Lequel par ces présentes constitué pour mandataire:

Monsieur [*name, occupation and address of attorney*]

A l'effet de recueillir la succession de Monsieur/Madame [*surname and first name*], [*profession*], demeurant en son vivant à [*lifetime address*] époux/épouse/veuf/veuve de [*name of surviving or pre-deceased spouse*], de nationalité [*nationality*], né [*date and place of birth*] et décédé à [*date and place of death*]

En consequence:

REQUERIR toutes appositions de scellés ou s'y opposer, en demander la levée avec ou sans description, faire procéder à tous inventaires des biens dépendant de la succession dont il s'agit, rectifications et récolements; dans le cours de ces opérations faire tous dires, déclarations, réquisitions, protestations et réserves, donner toutes dispenses, introduire tous référés ou y defendre, demander toutes autorisations pour agir sans attribution de qualités, faire nommer tous administrateurs ou s'opposer à leur nomination, choisir tous gardiens et dépositaires;

PRENDRE connaissance des forces et charges de cette succession, l'accepter purement et simplement ou sous bénéfice d'inventaire ou meme y renoncer, faire à cet effet toutes déclarations;

CONSENTIR ou contester l'exécution de tous actes de liberalité, en faire ou accepter la délivrance, demander ou consentir toutes réductions;

REQUERIR toute attestation de transmission de tous droits réels immobiliers;

FAIRE procéder avec ou sans attribution de qualité à la vente des objets mobiliers, en toucher le prix, faire toutes acquisitions;

GERER et administrer les biens dépendant de la succession dont il s'agit, passer et résilier tous baux et locations, demander ou consentir toutes prorogations, faire exécuter toutes réparations, arrêter tous devis et conventions;

RECEVOIR ou payer toutes sommes en principal, intérêts et accessoires pouvant être dues à tel titre et pour quelque cause que ce soit, proposer ou accepter toute imputation, compensation ou confusion;

REQUERIR tous certificats de propriété, faire toutes déclarations de non-cumul, requérir toutes attestations de transmission d'immeuble et publications;

ACQUITTER tous droits de mutation, faire toutes déclarations, faire toutes demandes en obtention de délai, prendre à cet effet tous engagements envers le Trésor et constituer à son profit toutes garanties, faire toutes demandes en remise ou en restitution, signer toutes déclarations, certifier tous états, faire toutes renociations à des créances, toucher le montant de toutes remises ou restitutions;

TOUCHER et recevoir de la Banque de France, de la Caisse des Dépôts et Consignations ainsi que de toutes banques ou de tous tiers quelconques toutes sommes valeurs et objets dépendant de la succession dont il s'agit, opérer tous retraits, en donner décharge, faire tous dépôts de sommes et de valeurs;

REPRESENTER le constituant à toutes assemblées de copropriétaires;

RETIRER de la poste tous plis, paquets et lettres chargés ou non;

ARRETER tous comptes avec tous créanciers, débiteurs,

dépositaires et tiers quelconques, en fixer les réliquats, les recevoir ou payer;

ETABLIR tous comptes de bénéfice d'inventaire et procéder à toutes distributions entre les créanciers;

VENDRE et céder, soit de gré à gré, soit par adjudication, tout ou partie des biens ou droits mobiliers ou immobiliers dépendant de la succession dont il s'agit aux prix charges et conditions que le mandataire avisera, toucher le prix, soit comptant soit aux termes convenus, nommer tous séquestres, faire toutes indication de paiement, consentir toutes délégations aux créanciers inscrits, acquérir tout ou partie de ces biens ou droits, en payer le prix;

OBLIGER le constituant conjointement et solidairement avec tous covendeurs à toutes garanties ordinaires et de droits et au rapport de toutes justifications et mainlevées et de tous certificats de radiation:

FAIRE toutes déclarations d'état civil et autres;

DE toutes sommes reçues ou payées, donner ou retirer quittances et décharges, reconnaître tous paiements antérieurs, consentir toutes mentions et subrogations avec ou sans garantie, faire mainlevée et consentir la radiation avec désistement de tous droits de privilège, hypothèque, action résolutoire de toutes inscriptions ou saisies oppositions et autres empêchements quelconques, le tout avec ou sans constation de paiement, consentir ou accepter toutes antériorités et toutes restrictions de privilège ou hypothèques, faire et accepter toutes offres et consignations, opérer le retrait de toutes sommes consignées, remettre ou se faire remettre tous titres et pièces, retirer ou donner toutes décharges;

AUX effets ci-dessus passer et signer tous actes, procés-verbaux et pièces, élire domicile, substituer avec faculté pour les mandataires de faire toutes substitutions et généralement faire le nécessaire.

DONT ACTE EN BREVET
Etabli en – pages
FAIT ET PASSE A –

Certificats de Coutume

The following precedents may be given in French or in English (in which case they will require translating) by a person suitably qualified in English law, who will normally be a Solicitor or Member of the Bar. The certificate, which is the equivalent of an Affidavit of Foreign Law, does not need to be sworn or to be in the form of a Statutory Declaration. The precedent given here is for a sale but can very simply be adapted for a purchase. Clause 4 assumes a fairly standard objects clause in the Memorandum of Association of the English company involved and Clause 6 assumes that it is a pre-1985 company to which the 1985 Table A applies. Slight alterations may have to be made to the precedent in the case of a company which takes advantage of any of the simplifications (e.g. in paragraph 4 if it has a short form of Memorandum) available under the Companies Act 1989.

Sometimes a Notary will insist on a complete copy with translation of the Memorandum and Articles of Association of the selling or buying company. This is not necessary, as all that is needed to prove the power of the company to sell or buy land or indeed any other asset in France is contained in the Certificate which in the form of this precedent is acceptable to the various *Conservateurs des Hypothèques* to whom it has been submitted. There are, however, at least 150 local Land Registry offices, and it is wise to submit the document in draft form to the Notary concerned. On occasion, a very much shorter *Certificat de Coutume* may be acceptable; its acceptance probably depends in no small measure on the extent of the Notary's knowledge of English law.

A precedent in this short form is included for use in connection with an English company's subscription for shares in a new SARL, but it can be adapted for sale or purchase of land or other assets.

Je soussigné, [*name*], [*qualification*], demeurant à [*address*] VU:
    une copie conforme du Certificat de Constitution [*Certificate of Incorporation*] de la société de droit anglais XYZ LIMITED;
    des copies conformes de l'acte de constitution [*Memorandum of Association*] et les statuts [*Articles of Association*] de ladite société;
    les registres concernant ladite société que ladite société est tenue de garder;
    une copie conforme d'un procés verbal d'une réunion des administrateurs de ladite société tenue le [*date of board meeting*]
    les lois et coutumes anglaises en matière de sociétés;
ET ATTENDU:
1. Que le Certificat de Constitution sus-visé fait foi en droit anglais de la constitution sous la forme de société à responsabilité

limitée par actions [*company limited by shares*] de XYZ LIMITED.

2. Que toute société de droit anglais est constituée pour une durée illimitée sauf dissolution volontaire ou forcée et le Greffier des Sociétés [*Registrar of Companies*] a confirmé qu'il n'y a aucune inscription dans les registres tenus sous sa garde tendant à une telle dissolution.

3. Que le siège social de ladite société est sis à [*address of registered office*], Angleterre, le capital de ladite société est de £   divisé en actions de £   chacune et que les administrateurs sont [*names of directors*].

4. Que l'acte constitutif de la société qui n'a subi aucune modification depuis son adoption fait apparaître que les objets pour lesquels la société a été constituée comprennent celui de: '3. (–) vendre ou par tout autre moyen aliéner en totalité ou en partie ... les biens des la société moyennant un prix que la société jugera convenable' de sorte que rien n'empêche en droit anglais que ladite société poursuit ses affaires dans le cadre de ses objets et vend ses biens immobiliers à l'étranger.

5. Que les statuts de la société font apparaître que la société est gérée par un conseil d'administration dont le nombre sera déterminé par la société en assemblée générale et qui est actuellement composé des personnes visées sous la rubrique 3 ci-dessus.

6. Que les pouvoirs du conseil d'administration de la société sont ceux visés aux articles du 'Table A' qui fait partie du décret S.I. N.°.85/805 (modifié ensuite par le décret S.I. N°85/1502) qui a modifié les articles des parties I et II du 'Table A' du Companies Act 1948 réputées reproduits aux statuts en vertu de l'article 1 desdits statuts, à savoir – 'les articles contenus ou incorporés aux parties I et II de la Table A dans le premier annexe au Companies Act 1948 ... s'appliqueront à la société sauf s'ils ont été exclus ou transformés et lesdits articles (sauf exclusion et transformation) et les articles ci-après contenus seront les règlementations de la société.'

7. Qu'en vertu de l'Article 71 dudit 'Table A' également réputé reproduit aux statuts de la société 'le conseil d'administration pourra par procuration ou par tout autre moyen nommer toute personne mandataire de la société avec de tels pouvoirs et sous telles conditions qu'ils jugeront utiles y compris le pouvoir de délégation'

8. Que selon la Loi sur les sociétés de 1985 la copie conforme du procès-verbal dont un exemplaire traduit en langue française demeure annexée à la procuration en date du [*date of power of attorney*] signée par ledit M [*name of donor of power authorized*

by the board resolution] au nom de la société délivré sous la signature d'un des administrateurs ou du secrétaire ou de toute autre personne dument autorisée par la société doit être reçu comme faisant foi de son contenu.

JE SOUSSIGNE CERTIFIE ET ATTESTE:

Que XYZ Limited est une société anglaise régulièrement constituée et toujours en existence, ayant les siège social, capital, administrateurs et objets ci-dessus visés, ayant valablement délibéré de vendre un bien immeuble en France soit [*short description of property to be sold*] et d'autoriser un de ses administrateurs ledit Monsieur [*donor of the power*] de signer et passer au nom de la société une procuration pour la vente dudit appartement et généralement faire tout ce qui sera nécessaire à cet effet.

EN FOI DE QUOI je délivre le présent certificat de coutume pour servir et valoir ce que de droit.

Le [*date*] 19–.

SHORT FORM OF *CERTIFICAT DE COUTUME*

JE SOUSSIGNE, [*name*], [*qualification*], demeurant à [*address*]

CERTIFIE ET ATTESTE à la vue des documents constitutifs de la société XYZ LIMITED et spécialement de ses statuts.

QUE ladite société est régulièrement constituée pour une durée illimitée selon le droit anglais, qu'elle a la capacité juridique et peut valablement participer à la constitution d'une société à responsabilité limitée de droit français

QUE la décision du Conseil d'Administration de ladite société en date du — 19- a été prise conformément aux lois anglaises et aux statuts de ladite société

QUE Monsieur ABC [*the person named in the board resolution*] a tous les pouvoirs pour engager valablement ladite société et généralement faire tout ce qui sera utile ou nécessaire

FAIT à — le — 19-.

Wills and Successions

The cases in which English practitioners are involved in obtaining an English Grant of Representation to deal with assets in the UK based solely on a French Will or on the intestacy of a person who died domiciled in France will be comparatively rare. Such a situation requires an Affidavit of French Law to submit with the other papers to lead to the grant. The Probate Registry are both extremely helpful and extremely knowledgeable where questions of foreign succession law are concerned. However expert the maker of the Affidavit of French law may be, it is generally safer to submit it for consideration to the Registry in draft form before it is finally sworn. The following precedent, which in its alternative paragraphs takes account of both a Will made in holograph style according to French law and a Will executed in accordance with the requirements of English law, is included out of general interest.

IN THE HIGH COURT OF JUSTICE
FAMILY DIVISION
THE PRINCIPAL REGISTRY

IN the Estate of —— deceased.
I —— of —— make oath and say as follows:
1. I am conversant with the laws of France having [*insert here a suitable qualification or a suitable explanation of the deponent's expertise such as 'for the last — years I have advised on and been involved in many cases of persons not of French nationality who have died domiciled in France leaving Wills executed according to the laws of their nationality and in particular in cases of persons of British nationality dying in such circumstances*].
2. I have referred to the last Will and Testament of [*name and address of deceased*] deceased bearing date the — 19- a true copy of which is now produced to me marked 'A'.
3. I know that the said deceased was at all times during his life a British subject and that he had for many years been domiciled in France and died domiciled in that country.
4. [*If the deceased left a French holograph Will:*] In my opinion, the said Will is valid according to the laws of France. Article 969 of the French Civil Code permits a Testator to make a Will in one of three forms, of which one is the holograph Will. Article 970 of the said Code says (in translation) 'A holograph Will shall not be valid unless its entire contents and date and signature are in the handwriting of the testator; it is subject to no other formality.' The said Will is so written dated and signed.
OR
4. [*If the deceased left a Will executed in English form:*] It is a rule of French law as to the formal validity of a Will made by a person not of French nationality who dies domiciled in France that it is treated as properly executed if its execution conforms (if it does not conform to the laws of France) to the laws of the

country of the Testator's nationality. This rule stems from judicial interpretations of Article 999 of the French Civil Code. The commentary on this Article in the Seventh edition of Batiffol and Legarde on 'Droit International Privé' (which is a standard textbook on the subject) reads (in translation) as follows: 'Insofar as Wills are concerned ... jurisprudence has interpreted its text as applying a general rule permitting a Testator of French nationality to execute a Will abroad in a form recognized as valid by local law and by way of reciprocity, recognizing as valid in form Wills of foreigners executed in accordance with the requirements of the law of their nationality.' The said Will being executed in accordance with the requirements of English law consequently is recognized as properly executed by the internal law in force in the territory where it was executed, namely France.

5. In these circumstances, the requirements of Section 1 of the Wills Act 1963 are fulfilled and the said Will should for the reasons stated above be treated as properly executed for the purpose of obtaining Probate thereof in England.

SWORN etc.

The following precedent for a holograph Will is included as a matter of interest only, which explains the apparent catholicity of the dispositions.

Ceci est mon testament.
Je soussigné [*name, address and occupation*] révoque toutes dispositions antérieures aux présents.
[*Gift of whole estate to a single beneficiary – légataire universel.*]
Je déclare léguer à mon [*relationship and name, address and occupation of legatee*] tous les bien meubles et immeubles qui composeront ma succession sans exception ni réserve et en conséquence je l'institue mon légataire universel.
[*Gift of whole estate to several beneficiaries – légataires universels – with substitution and accruer provision*]
Je déclare instituer pour mes légataires universels conjointement entre eux [*relationships, names, addresses and occupations of beneficiaries*]. Si l'un d'entre eux vient à mourir avant moi sa part reviendra à ses enfants (légitimes) suivant les régles de la représentation. A défaut de descendants (légitimes) la part du légataire décédé accroîtra aux survivants.
[*Gift of all estate to surviving spouse subject to such reduction as may have to be made to satisfy* héritiers réservataires, *the choice of how the remaining interest will be ascertained being left to the surviving spouse*]

Je déclare instituer ma femme/mon mari [*name and date and place of birth*] pour mon/ma légataire universel[le] en pleine propriété. Au cas où la réduction de ce legs serait demandée par les héritiers réservataires qui existeraient au jour de mon décès j'entends que mon mari/ma femme bénéficie de la plus grande quotité disponible permise entre époux par la loi soit en pleine propriété ou en usufruit seulement soit en pleine propreiété et en usufruit au choix exclusif de mon mari/ma femme. Si je laisse un ou plusieurs ascendants venant à ma succession la part de mon mari/ma femme comprendra la nue-propriété de la réserve légale des ascendants. (Pour les biens dont il/elle aura l'usufruit je le/la dispense de faire emploi et de fournir caution mais il/elle devra dresser inventaire)

[*Gift of specified part of estate to a beneficiary – légataire à titre universel*]

Je déclare léguer à [*name, address and occupation of beneficiary*] tous les biens et droits mobiliers que je laisserai à mon décès et qui feront partie de ma succession sans en rien excepter ni réserver.

[*Gift of farm to a single beneficiary*]

Je légue à [*name, address and occupation*] la ferme de – située à [*address*] telle qu'elle existera à mon décès avec le chaptel et les immeubles par destination en dépendant et avec droit aux revenus à compter de mon décès sans avoir en demander la délivrance

[*Specific legacy – legs particulier*]

Je déclare léguer à [*name, address and profession of beneficiary*] [*description of particular item bequeathed*] que je possède situé à [*address where item is*]

[*Legacy for upkeep of grave*]

Je légue au bureau de bienfaisance de — [*or other appropriate legatee*] la somme de – francs dont les revenus devront servir d'abord à entretenir à perpetuité ma tombe au cimetière de [*place*] (et pour le surplus être distribué aux pauvres de —). La somme ainsi léguée sera employée à l'achat de [*a suitable investment, presumably French, such as a 'titre de rente sur l'Etat français'*].

[*Appointment of Exécuteur Testamentaire*]

Je nomme pour exécuteur testamentaire [*name, address and occupation*] à qui je donne la saisine de tous mes biens meubles pendant l'année après mon décès. (Pour l'indemniser de tous ses soins je le prie d'accepter un diamant de [*amount*] francs net de tous frais et droits quelconques). [*It is possible to give further limited powers but these should not be granted without advice.*]

[*Form of execution of holograph Wills.*]
Fait écrit daté et signé entièrement de ma main à [*place of execution*] le [*date of execution in full and preferably all in words*] *AND NO WITNESSES*

CERTIFICAT DE COUTUME TO DEAL WITH FRENCH PERSONALTY

In the case of a person dying domiciled in England with personalty only in France and leaving only an English Will, the Executor(s) appointed by that Will will be accepted as competent in France to call in, sell and distribute that personalty. The Notary dealing with the estate in France will require a *Certificat de Coutume* made by an English lawyer, who will presumably be the Solicitor acting in the estate in England. A typical certificate is shown below. It can be adapted to suit each case, including an intestacy, where it will have to be shown that the Administrators have the same powers as Executors. The certificate, which assumes that the Act and Will exhibited will be sealed certified copies (which is desirable), can be made in English and suitably translated or could, for example, be made originally in French by a Notary Public. On the whole, it is desirable that it be shown in draft form to the Notary involved, since some are much more *au fait* with the English system than others while some view it with utter disbelief.

Je soussigné [*name, address and qualification*]
ATTENDU le décès survenu le [*date of death*] de [*full name of deceased*] de nationalité [*nationality*] né à [*place of birth*] le [*date of birth*] en son vivant [*occupation of deceased*] demeurant à [*last address of deceased*] époux en uniques noces de Madame XYZ [*or such other état civil as may be correct, using the maiden name of the deceased's wife*] ayant nommé dans son testament en date du [*date of will*] ABC son exécuteur testamentaire ET VU la copie dudit testament du décédé et de l'ordonnance en date du [*date of grant*] les deux certifiées conformes par un des greffiers juges du Principal Probate Registry du Family Division de la Haute Cour de Justice en Angleterre.
CERTIFIE
1. La décédé était domicilé en Angleterre au moment de son décès et la loi successorale à laquelle est soumise sa succession est donc la loi anglaise.
2. Le loi anglaise donne à l'exécuteur testamentaire du moment

du décès du décédé et sans formalité la saisine de tous les biens meubles et immeubles qui composent sa succession et tous les pouvoirs pour les appréhender, vendre et distribuer. Ladite ordonnance du Tribunal ne fait que confirmer la nomination de l'exécuteur testamentaire.

3. Le décédé ne possédait que des biens mobiliers situés en France à savoir; [*set out items*].

4. Ledit Monsieur ABC l'exécuteur testamentaire nommé dans le testament dudit décédé a donc tous les pouvoirs nécessaires pour appréhender, vendre, reçevoir le prix de vente ou de distribuer les biens mobiliers précités composant [une partie de] la succession dudit décédé en France.

En foi de quoi j'ai délivré le présent certificat de coutume

Fait en brevet à mon étude à (Londres)

L'An mil neuf cent etc.

Certificat de Propriété for French car

The following precedent in connection with the transfer of a French-registered car has successfully been used in terms which deliberately avoid any reference to other estate in France. The Order of the Court to which it refers is, of course, the English grant, to which must be annexed the Will, since this will show the name of the specific legatee of the car or of the residuary legatee. The wording may well need altering to fit circumstances. For example, if there is an intestacy and therefore no Will in which a name for a new owner can figure, it would be as well to show the Administrators as the new owners and explain that under English law the Grant confirms their ownership. Executors will have to content themselves at being bypassed by this method, but it is worth while if a car is the only asset in France which needs dealing with. In such case there is no need to use the services of a Notary. Strictly speaking, French Consulates in the U.K. should be able to confirm that the Certificate is in proper order (this precedent is based on a Consular form) but it is not recommended that their services be used. French Consulates are apt to play the game very much by the rules and not always get the rules right, whereas the *Préfecture* of the *Departement* where the car was registered may well be more helpful and will certainly be correct in its requirements. It is there that a full draft should be taken for checking, often with useful results, by an intelligent but not necessarily legally qualified person. A *carte grise* is the car's logbook.

Je soussigné [*name, address and qualifications of the giver of the certificate*]
ATTENDU le décès survenu le [*date of death*] de [*full name of deceased*] de nationalité [*nationality*] né à [*place of birth*] le [*date of birth*] en son vivant [*occupation of deceased*] demeurant à [*last address of deceased*] époux en uniques noces de Madame XYZ [*or such other état civil as may be correct, using the maiden name of the deceased's wife*] ainsi qu'il est constaté dans l'ordonnance en date du [*date of grant*] du Principal [*District*] Probate Registry of the High Court of Justice in England
ET VU:
1. La carte grise de la voiture automobile dont l'immatriculation figure en tête des présentes;
2. Une expédition de l'acte de décès de Monsieur [*the name of the deceased*] susnommé délivré par [*the Registrar of Births, Deaths and Marriages at place of issue of death certificate*] et annexé à ces présentes avec une traduction en français certifié par le Consul britannique à [*place of consulate – or this may be translated by a Notary Public in Britain*];
3. Une copie certifiée conforme avec traduction en français certifié conforme par [*as in 2 above*] dudit ordonnance du tribunal britannique aux termes duquel [*name of the legatee or residuary beneficiary*] est confirmé comme légataire particulier/légataire universel de la succession en Angleterre dudit [*name of deceased*];
4. CERTIFIE que la voiture automobile susvisée appartient en toute propriété à ladite ABC
En foi de quoi j'ai délivré le présent certificat de propriété
Fait en brevet à mon étude à [*Londres*]
L'An mil neuf cent etc.

Appendix B: Rates of Duties and Land Registry and Notarial Fees

Rates of Droits de Succession
See note on page 193.

A. Beneficiary related in direct line to the deceased

Slice of estate	*Rate* %
Not exceeding 50,000 francs	5
50,000 to 75,000 francs	10
75,000 to 100,000 francs	15
100,000 to 3,400,000 francs	20
3,400,000 to 5,600,000 francs	30
5,600,000 to 11,200,000 francs	35
In excess of 11,200,000 francs	40

B. Beneficiary a surviving spouse

Slice of estate	*Rate* %
Not exceeding 50,000 francs	5
50,000 to 100,000 francs	10
100,000 to 200,000 francs	15
200,000 to 3,400,000 francs	20
3,400,000 to 5,600,000 francs	30
5,600,000 to 11,200,000 francs	35
In excess of 11,200,000 francs	40

The threshold for any beneficiary of the classes mentioned above is 275,000 francs, which is applicable to the benefit taken by *each* such beneficiary. Thus, in a net estate of 1,500,000 francs, in which a surviving spouse takes a quarter share and three surviving children each take a quarter share, duty will be payable by each beneficiary at the appropriate rate on the amount of 100,000 francs i.e. on 375,000 francs less 275,000 francs *abattement*. When issue take by representation the share of a predeceased child, the *abattement* is that to which the deceased child would have been entitled and is shared between the issue who take his share. An *abattement* wholly or partly applied for the benefit of a donee on a gift made to him *inter vivos* is taken into account in calculating the *abattement* available on the death of the donor.

When the beneficiary is a brother or sister the rate is:

On that part of the net estate not exceeding 150,000 francs	35%
On that part of the net estate exceeding 150,000 francs	45%

A special *abattement* of 100,000 francs is available in respect of the share of any brother or sister if he or she has never married or is a widower or widow or is divorced or judicially separated, provided he or she (a) is aged more than fifty at the date of death of the deceased or (b) suffers from some illness which prevents him or her from earning a livelihood *and* in either case continuously resided with the deceased for the period of five years ending with his death.

In the case of a beneficiary who is a relative of the deceased not of a class mentioned above but up to and including the fourth degree, the rate is 55%.

In the case of all more distant relatives or of 'strangers in blood', the rate is 60%.

The following *abattements* are also available:

(i) in all cases where no other *abattement* is available: 10,000 francs;

(ii) where any beneficiary, whether related or not to the deceased, is prevented by reason of a physical or mental disability from earning his living under normal conditions or, if he or she is under the age of eighteen, is for the same reasons unable to undergo normal training (which is not added to any other *abattement* to which he or she might be entitled by reason of relationship to the deceased): 300,000 francs;

(iii) if the beneficiary has three or more children living or the issue of three or more predeceased children living at the date of the deceased's death and:

(a) the beneficiary is the surviving spouse or is in direct line to the deceased, for each child or issue in excess of two: 4,000 francs;

(b) the deceased is otherwise related or is not related to the deceased, for each child or issue in excess of two: 2,000 francs;

(iv) a small reduction is made for the war-wounded whose invalidity exceeds fifty per cent.

Certain charitable bequests are free from *droits de succession*. Enquiries should be made in each case to establish whether a particular organization so benefits or not. English rules establishing 'charitableness' do not apply in France.

1. The Finance Law 1971 proposes that as from the 1 January 1992, the *abattement* for suriving spouses will be 330,000 francs and for ascendants and descendants will be 300,000 francs.

2. These *abattements* together with the *abattement* of 100,000 francs available in certain circumstances for brothers and sisters will, contrary to current rules, be cumulative with the *abattement* of 300,000 francs available for the physically or mentally handicapped.

Life interests and reversions are valued as follows:

Age of Life Tenant	*Value of Life Interest* %	*Value of Reversion* %
Not exceeding 21 years	70	30
Not exceeding 31 years	60	40
Not exceeding 41 years	50	50
Not exceeding 51 years	40	60
Not exceeding 61 years	30	70
Not exceeding 71 years	20	80
Exceeding 71 years	10	90

Rates of Droits de Donation

Basically, the same duties as are payable and the same *abattements* as are available on death are payable and available in respect of gifts *inter vivos*. There are certain small differences in the rules applicable to valuations, e.g. the

Revenue will accept on the making of a gift a valuation of jewellery provided that it is not less than sixty per cent of its insured value. Moreover, gift duty cannot be paid by instalments except in the case of a gift of a business or unquoted company which would qualify for the payment of duty by instalments on a death.

In addition, when the gift is by way of *donation-partage* i.e. a gift of property made by parents or other ascendants to children and descendants, there is a special reduction in the duty payable depending on the age of the donor at the date of making the gift. If the donor is aged sixty-five or less, the reduction is twenty-five per cent; if aged between sixty-five and seventy-five the reduction is fifteen per cent; there is no reduction if the donor is aged more than seventy-five.

Stamp Duties

The basic rate of stamp duty payable in respect of the conveyance of land is calculated as follows:

Départemental duty	13.8% + 1.6%	= 15.4%
Local tax		1.2%
Regional tax		1.6%
		————
		18.2%

The following are the reduced rates of stamp duty payable, the numbering corresponding to that in Chapter 21.

1. *Départemental* duty	4.2% + 1.6%	= 4.2%
Local tax		1.2%
Regional tax		1.6%
		————
		7.0%

2. A single duty of   0.6%

3. The overall duty is reduced by 2%, except in Corsica where the reduction is 7.9%

4. *Départemental* duty	4.8% + 1.6%	= 6.4%
Local tax		1.2%
Regional tax		1.6%
		————
		9.2%

5. *Départemental* duty   6.4% + 1.2%   =   7.6%
   Local tax   1.2%
   Regional tax   1.6%

                                                                10.4%

This reduced rate is limited to 650,000 francs of the price if this exceeds that amount.

6. A single duty of   0.6%

7. *Départemental* duty   2% + 1.6%   =   3.6%
   Local tax   1.2%
   Regional tax   1.6%

                                                                  6.4%

8. The *Départemental* duties vary from nil on, for example, property bought by the State and local authorities to 0.6 per cent for purchases by SAFER and by certain property companies as part of a lease-back operation and to six per cent for cultural and similar institutions and agricultural co-operatives.

NOTE

In all cases there must be added (for the benefit of the State) 2.5 per cent of the amount of the *Départemental* duty actually payable. The regional duties quoted above are those charged by the majority of the Regions but one or two charge less. The maximum which can be charged is 1.6%.

Land Registry Fees

Registration of transfers of
land or other interests in realty   0.1% of the
                                                     transfer price
Registration of charges etc   0.05% of amount
                                                     of loan
Cancellation of entries of charges etc   0.1% of value
Cancellation/variation of certain other
   entries   0.05% of value

Notarial Fees

Scale I given below represents profit costs pure and simple for the preparation of an *acte de vente* on the sale of real property. It does not include ancillary work, such as making Land Registry searches or clearing off entries and does not include disbursements, despite the fact that these costs and disbursements together are frequently referred to as *frais de notaire*. The scale shown produces figures to which TVA must be added.

Scale I

Slice of Price	Fee %	Cumulative Total
Up to 20,000 francs	5	1,000 francs
20,001 to 40,000 francs	3.3	+660 = 1,660 francs
40,001 to 110,000 francs	1.65	+1,155 = 2,815 francs
In excess of 110,000 francs	0.825	

The following scale is of commission charged by the Notary who has a *mandat* from his client to negotiate the sale of property. The resultant fee is, unless otherwise agreed between seller and buyer, considered to be part of the *frais d'acte* and therefore paid by the buyer.

Scale II

Slice of Price	Fee %
Up to FF175,000	5
Above FF175,000	2.5

A Notary may not share a Scale I fee with any person but may in certain circumstances share a Scale II fee with certain persons.

Appendix C: Exempt Non-French Companies

The following is a list of some of the countries with which France has a Tax Treaty which includes provisions for exchange of information with a view to the repression of tax evasion. See page 73.

All Common Market countries
Australia
Austria
Canada
Cyprus
Czechoslovakia
Finland
Hungary
Israel
Japan
Norway
New Zealand
Poland
Monaco
Malta
Singapore
Sweden
Switzerland*
United States

* A most significant decision of the Cour de Cassation of 21 December 1990 confirms that companies whose seat of management is in Switzerland are exempt from the 3% tax. Liechtenstein is *not* Switzerland. It remains to be seen whether the Revenue will accept this decision which it is not incapable of ignoring.

Appendix D: Table of Statutes and Statutory Instruments

Glossary

In this book, every effort has been made to keep the use of legal terms to a minimum. Where it is necessary to refer to a document or a process by name, in the majority of cases the appropriate French term is used, sometimes with its English translation or equivalent rather than its English translation alone. It has been thought useful to collect some of these terms in this glossary and to include some which may not appear in the body of the book.

The choice of what words or expressions should be included in the glossary is not whimsical and it is intended to cover most of the situations in connection with property or probate matters which will present themselves to readers. It cannot, however, take account of the extent of each reader's knowledge of French. Although not a few English legal terms retain their Norman-French flavour, few, if any, would be comprehensible to the present-day French lawyer. By the same token, a number of old French legal terms still in use in France seem never to have found their way, corrupt or incorrupt, into current English legal usage. The only way of being certain that the translation of a legal term is correct is to have a reasonable working knowledge of the law of both countries involved or to consult someone who has; in the long run, it is safe to rely only on that method of discovering the true import of a document written in a foreign language and subject to a foreign legal system.

There are Anglo-French legal dictionaries available but their use by anyone not already reasonably conversant with both English and French legal language can be dangerous. A very useful legal dictionary is *Le Dictionnaire Juridique* by Bleyte, Kurgansky, Laroche and Spindler (Editions de Navarre, Paris), which is probably not readily available in Britain but can certainly be ordered through suitable booksellers. It has, however, for the English practitioner, the disadvantage that there is a slight tendency towards the use of expressions and procedures which are more familiar on the other side of the Atlantic; it is not always totally accurate and does suffer from a few surprising lacunae. It is nevertheless remarkably comprehensive and useful. A much shorter dictionary is *Le Dictionnaire Commerciale et Financier* by J.V. Servotte (Editions Marabout, Verviers, Belgium). This book is available in the United Kingdom. Although strictly it is a commercial dictionary, it contains a considerable number of legal commercial and banking terms and it is one of the most useful and accurate of its size.

It would be very helpful if the English distinction between documents executed under hand and under seal could be applied to the distinction between French documents which are on the one hand executed *sous seign privé* and on the other hand are *actes notariés* or *actes authentiques*, but it cannot. The distinction in France is simply that documents signed *sous seign privé* ('s.s.p.' as they are frequently referred to and are so called in this book) are documents which are not signed before a Notary. An *acte notarié or acte authentique*, as the name implies, requires execution by all parties in the presence of a Notary. Certain documents are required by French law to be notarial documents but many may be in the form of *acte authentique* or may be executed s.s.p. To some extent, notarial execution implies the solemnity which is given to English deeds as opposed to documents under hand but documents for signature s.s.p. are not infrequently drafted by Notaries. But the basic reason for the involvement of the Notary is to make the document one of public record, the date, execution and contents of which cannot (except as to matters of construction) be called into question. Moreover, French law naturally knows nothing of English rules of contract and of the use of the deed to effect a valid transaction where no consideration passes.

All French documents, of whatever kind, are or should be initialled by all the parties on each page as well as being signed on the last page. There is, of course, except in the case of a Will, no need to have witnesses to an *acte authentique*, nor are witnesses required for documents executed s.s.p. The former will always show the number of pages, strikings-out and alterations; the latter will frequently show these. If it is asked why there should be a standard provision for amendments to documents and why documents are not necessarily in their final form prior to execution, the answer is that it is far from infrequent for alterations and additions to be made at the moment of execution, and this can stem only from the difference in the relationship between Solicitor and client and Notary and client and from the fact that often only one Notary is involved.

Many s.s.p. documents contain a *mention* in the handwriting of the party (parties) in such form as the very common '*vu et lu*' or '*lu et approuvé*'.

There are *mentions* to meet most occasions, such as '*bon pour vente*' or '*bon pour pouvoir*'. Strictly speaking, an Attorney should sign his Power with appropriate words that he accepts the appointment. With one exception (see below), there seems no statutory requirement for this almost universally used method of signature. It may well be that there is truth in the suggestion to be found in one French precedent book that, in cases where the authenticity of a signature is in issue, it may be difficult to prove a mere signature but that a few words added in the handwriting of the signatory may render this task easier. Whatever the truth of the matter may be, most people will be unhappy at a signature without the appropriate preceding magic words.

Article 1326 of the Code Civil as originally drawn required that, in the case of certain unilateral contracts for the benefit of a person not a party to the contract, the executing party add in his own handwriting '*un bon ou un approuvé*' and the amount involved in words. As a matter of history only, for this Article has been repealed and replaced by another, this provision did not apply to 'tradesmen, artisans, labourers, workers in vineyards, day workers or servants'. The new Article, which took effect in July 1980, now requires that in such contracts the amount of money or the value of the consideration appear in words and figures in the handwriting of the executing party. Such a rule applies of course only to documents s.s.p. and insofar as conveyancing documents are concerned ostensibly only to *promesses de vente*, since the *compromis de vente* is bilateral. Even so, there is doubt whether this Article applies even in the case of *promesses de vente* where the amount of money involved can be considered not to be the primary subject of the contract but rather as subsidiary to a larger engagement, i.e. the transfer of property.

It is not possible to become involved in any transaction in France without encountering the expression '*état civil*'. It is the description of a private person by reference to his parentage, his date and place of birth, his date and place of marriage, the *régime matrimonial* under which he was married, his divorce and remarriage, his nationality etc. A woman is known by her maiden name, 'wife of' her husband. Breaking with long tradition, a woman who is a mother and housewife may describe her occupation as '*mère au foyer*' instead of '*sans*'; this is considered to be a significant step along the road to emancipation.

In the case of the non-French, the Notary and other authorities frequently rely on their passports or (if they have them) national identity cards for such of this information as can be gleaned from them. Sometimes birth, death and marriage certificates are required. When they are, it is self-evident that translations are needed. In certain cases, in an effort to fit in with the French system, it is required that such certificates be not more than three months old. This means that the certified copy of the English entry of the relevant event must have been issued not more than three months before its use, and it is quite useless explaining that such a certified copy issued many years previously is equally valid as proof of the event related in it. The problem by no means always arises, but when it does (often with the Companies Registries), there is no alternative but to get a 'new' certificate.

It must be said that proof of identity, which never seems to cause much of a problem in the UK, takes on a much more serious and somewhat chauvinistic aspect in France, and sometimes the requirements of the 'Administration' can be extremely irritating. How the problem is dealt with depends much on the Notary involved: he will either cling to the straight and narrow and insist on what is asked for or take a somewhat wider view and make efforts to talk the authorities out of production of what may well not exist out of France in a form required by the French.

It is not necessary to elaborate the reference to French *régimes matrimoniaux* made in the body of this book. The use of an English Marriage Settlement is not the same as being married under a French matrimonial régime, if only because the French have no trust law, and any lucky beneficiary under such a Settlement whose Trustees buy property for his occupation in France should warn them to take most careful advice. He should without such advice having been obtained, avoid disclosing the fiduciary nature of the proposed purchasers. The problems which can arise if French property is in fact bought with English trust moneys is discussed elsewhere in this book. However, it is desirable to make certain that documents under which an English husband and/or wife buy property show that they have no *régime matrimonial* according to English law and what is the effect of this translated into French terms. An incorrect recital may result in a Notary taking the point that they *must* have such a *régime* with certain irritating consequences. In no event should English husbands and wives be shown as bound by the *régime matrimonial* imposed by the Married Women's Property Act, 1882 (as has appeared in more than one *acte*). The desirable description is: A and B *'mariés sous le régime anglais équivalent au régime français de la séparation de biens à défaut de contrat de marriage préalable à leur union célébrée le [date] à [place of marriage].'*

The following are some legal terms which are used in this book or which the reader may come across in French documents.

Abattement Fiscal relief giving rise to reduction in death duties or other taxes.

Acte de vente This may be safely translated as a conveyance. Land and other interests in realty may only be transferred by such a document. The document is usually *'de vente'*, whether looked at from the vendor's or purchaser's side.

Acte de notoriété après décès A notarial document which serves substantially the same purpose as a Grant of Representation except that it proves the title of individual beneficiaries and not of an Executor or Administrator.

Arrhes A deposit paid on exchange but which by virtue of Article 1,590 of the Code Civil has special significance. See Chapter 3.

Auteur A somewhat misleading term meaning a deceased person. Its use in, for example, Article 759 of the Code Civil could lead to misunderstanding if its true meaning were not appreciated.

Avancement d'hoirie An advancement made *inter vivos* which must be brought into hotchpot in the estate of the person making the advancement by the recipient. The word *hoirie* alone signifies 'the estate of', so that one finds, for example, a sale by *Hoirie Dupont*. See also *Préciput*.

Ayant-cause or *ayant-droit* In its widest sense, a successor in title. More narrowly used to mean persons entitled to share in (the residue of) an estate.

Bail Lease.

Cadastre One of the two parts of the French Land Registration system for the purpose of levying tax on registered owners.

Certificat de coutûme Affidavit of (foreign) law.

Clause d'accroissement See *Tontine*.

Compromis de vente A bilateral contract involving a binding agreement to buy and sell land. Sometimes (but rarely by the layman) called a *promesse synallagmatique de vente*.

Concurrence In its conveyancing sense means that there are two Notaries involved in a sale and the Notary who will not '*recoit l'acte*' is in *concurrence*. One finds also that the *acte* will be 'received' by Me. X 'with the assistance of' Me. Y.

Conservateur des hypothèques A District Land Registrar the information on whose registers, together with the information on the *Cadastre* (q.v.), is the equivalent (but with much missing material) of what is disclosed by an English Land Certificate.

Contrat de réservation The contract which it is required by law that every seller *en l'état futur* should enter into with the purchaser. Sometimes called a *contrat préliminaire*.

Copropriété Condominium.

Cridon A group of super-Notaries who advise their brother Notaries on difficult points of law. As near as can be, an opinion of *Cridon* is an Opinion of Counsel – limited to questions of notarial law. On the whole, its knowledge of

French Private International Law is excellent and Me. Marie-L. Revillard's 'feel' for English Wills and Trusts is exceptional.

Déclaration de succession Estate Duty Account (or whatever it may from time to time be called).

Décret Also known as *Décret-Loi* but now as *Ordonnance*. It may be compared practically but not constitutionally with a Statutory Instrument.

De cujus The deceased – testate or intestate.

Dedit Penalty provided for in a contract in the event of the default of one or either party.

Diamant The legacy given to an exécuteur testamentaire.

Dispense de rapport See *Préciput*

Donation Gift *inter vivos*.

D'ordre public A statutory requirement which cannot lawfully be varied or contracted out of *inter partes*. It also can mean 'law and order' but not in this book.

Droits de donation *Inter vivos* gifts tax.

Droit de passage Right of way.

Droits de succession Inheritance Tax or its equivalent under some other name.

Election de domicile The address for service of the parties to an *acte* which is usually for the non-French at the *étude* of the Notary receiving the *acte*. If two Notaries are involved, each party will usually *élire domicile* at the address of his Notary.

Emoluments A Notary's fee fixed according to scale.

Enregistrement Stamp duties. Sometimes used as Stamp Duty Office.

Etat hypothécaire Land Registry Search.

Exécuteur testamentaire Not the equivalent of the English Executor. See Chapter 17 as to his powers and duties.

Fente The division of the ascendants of a deceased person into the maternal and the paternal lines.

Frais de notaire The total costs of a notarial transaction including the Notary's fee, Stamp Duty and other relevant disbursements. Also known as *frais d'acte*.

Honoraires A Notary's (or other professional's) fee the amount of which is not fixed by scale.

Hors vue de notaire A payment, usually a purchase price, is so made when it does not pass through the Notary's clients' account but is paid direct from buyer to seller.

Huissier An officer of the Court who is akin to a Bailiff or Sheriff. He usually has some kind of legal qualification. He serves Writs, Court Orders, *Saisies*. He will also, for a fee, prepare statements of fact (*constats d'huissier*) the veracity of which is unassailable. Hence, if one suffers damage at the hands of another, a *constat d'huissier* will provide irrefutable evidence against disbelieving insurance companies. He also prepares Schedules of Condition and Dilapidations and serves Notices to Quit and many other documents which by law only he can serve. A very useful gentleman, particularly if he is on your side.

Hypothèque Mortgage.

Inventaire The inventory of all the assets of a deceased person which in certain cases it is obligatory to prepare.

Jouissance (entrée en) Taking possession.

Légataire universel A residuary legatee.

Légataire à titre universel Legatee of a specified proportion of an estate.

Légataire à titre particulier Pecuniary or specific legatee.

Lésion A particular kind of loss suffered by those who sell land at a considerable undervalue giving rise to the right to rescind the sale. It is not uninteresting to speculate why the framers of the Code Civil thought it necessary to include such a provision since it has remained unaltered since 1804.

Licitation Sale by auction of property held *en indivision*.

Lotissement Loosely but not too inadequately translated as a building/housing estate. Usually, there is an element of *copropriété* involved.

Loyer Rent reserved by a lease.

Mainlevée Release of a mortgage, charge, *saisie* etc.

Mandant/Mandataire The donor/donee of a Power of Attorney or similar authority.

Mettre en demeure To serve notice. Usually used with aggressive or contentious intent as a warning that proceedings may follow if the terms are not complied with, e.g. a notice to complete a purchase, a notice by a creditor to a debtor to pay. The notice itself is a *mise en demeure*.

Nue-propriété The reversion to property subject to a life interest.

Ordonnance The judgment of a Court. Also the name by

which under the current constitution the *décret* (q.v.) is now known.

Ouverture de la succession The estate of a deceased person is somewhat starkly described by the Code Civil as being 'opened' by his death. In rather wider terms, it refers to all the preliminary steps taken in connection with the estate of a deceased person.

Personne morale A corporate entity, including *sociétés civiles* (q.v.) as opposed to *personne physique* or individual person.

Préciput An advance is made '*par préciput et hors part*' or '*avec dispense de rapport*' when the recipient of the advance is relieved from the need to bring into hotchpot. It must be appreciated that, because of the rules relating to the *réserve*, this relief from bringing into hotchpot relates only to that part of an estate which may freely be disposed of by the Testator/Donor, so that, if the advance were to exceed that part of the estate not subject to the *réserve*, the excess would be subject to hotchpot.

Prêt Relais Bridging loan. Liable to be expensive as it is not unknown for the lender to take a charge both on the property to be sold and on the property bought.

Prime Insurance policy premium.

Procuration A Power of Attorney but frequently used for a somewhat more informal authority. Also known as a *Mandat* or *Pouvoir*.

Promesse de vente A unilateral agreement to sell land subject to the exercise by the purchaser of an option to buy contained in the agreement.

Publicité foncière Registration of a transaction, e.g. a sale.

Foncier – that which pertains to land. See *taxe foncière*.

Quittance Receipt.

Quotité disponible That part of an estate not within the *réserve*.

Rapporter à la masse successorale To bring into hotchpot. Hence *dipense de rapport* is a direction negativing hotchpot. See *Préciput*.

Recevoir un acte The Notary, before a document is executed, 'receives' or authenticates it. It is not always possible so to organize it, sometimes for good and sometimes for less good reasons, but if it can be arranged that it is the buyer's Notary who 'receives' the *acte de vente*, this is desirable. Among other things, it will then be he who deals with the registration of the transaction.

Rente viagère Annuity.

Réserve legal That part of a deceased's estate in which his surviving ascendants or descendants have entrenched inheritance rights.

Résolution Recission. Hence *clause résolutoire*, the provision in a contract dealing with circumstances in which it may be rescinded and *action en résolution* or recission suit.

Saisie arrêt Execution/attachment.

Saisie immobilière Charging Order on land.

Saisie conservatoire Somewhat akin in its effect to a Maraeva Order granted *ex parte* to block all assets of a reputed debtor. By no means infrequently resorted to in a wide variety of cases.

Saisine In succession cases, the right of the heir(s) to take possession of the assets of the deceased and to exercise all rights vested in him at his death. Effectively, the ownership which vests in an English Executor.

Servitude Easement.

Se porter fort To undertake on behalf of another; sometimes to act 'for and on behalf of' another. Also used in purchase contracts, where a purchaser may contract for himself and also '*en se portant fort*' for his assignees. Such use indicates that the ultimate purchaser will probably not be the contracting purchaser.

Société anonyme A public company (more or less).

Société à responsibility limitée A private company (more or less).

Société civile (professionnelle) A company by French legal standards but more akin to an English partnership. A *société civile professionnelle* (SCP as it is frequently called) is a partnership of 'professionals', which includes Notaries, Members of a Bar (*Avocats*) and Doctors and also those who possibly would not qualify as 'professionals' in the UK.

Soulte In connection with land transactions, a payment by way of equality of exchange and in succession matters, a payment made by one beneficiary to one or more other beneficiaries to achieve equality in a distribution.

Syndic The Managing Agent appointed by and to manage a *copropriété*.

Taxe foncière Land Tax levied locally on owners of property in each locality.

Taxe d'habitation Local Tax levied by the Local Authority on occupiers of properties in their area.

Tontine The equivalent in French law of ownership in joint tenancy. Purchase *en tontine* is frequently called a purchase *avec clause d'accroissement*.

TVA French VAT

Urbanisme Planning.

Usufruit Life interest.

Vente à rémeré Sale subject to a right of repurchase.

Index